From The Rat Race to Real Estate

The beginner's bible to real estate investing

Timothy Spangler

JRT Publishing Group - Plainfield, Illinois

From The Rat Race to Real Estate
The beginner's bible to real estate investing
by Timothy Spangler

Published by:
JRT Publishing Group
Post Office Box 192
Plainfield, IL 60544

jrtpublishing@comcast.net

ISBN, print edition   0-9766081-0-3

Printed in the United States of America

Library of Congress Control Number: 2005901524

Dedication

This book is dedicated to my lovely wife, Rosa, and my daughters Jessica and Jillian for their support, patience, and understanding. Thank you to my parents and my parents-in-law for their encouragement and unconditional love.

Acknowledgements

I would like to thank my friend Jake Mielnik for opening my eyes to the possibilities of real estate. Also, I would like to extend my appreciation to all of the people listed below for their hard work and expertise in the making of this book.

Cover design by Gregory Calvert

Editing by Hayden Writing Consultants

Forms by The Landlord Protection Agency

Printing by McNaughton & Gunn, Inc.

Contents

Legal Disclaimer

1

Overcoming the Rat Race

If you are reading this book, you've realized you're tired of the same old rat race day after day. You're ready for a change and ready to take charge of your destiny.

A few years ago, I was in the same predicament. I knew there had to be a way to make money where I didn't have a boss breathing down my neck. I wanted to avoid working for a company that found my services were no longer needed due to my age and get out of a situation where my retirement package might not have any money left in it when I was ready to retire, especially since Social Security isn't something people can count on for the future.

The more I considered being an employee, the more I realized working for someone else didn't offer much financial security. It is no fault of their own that most people end up working for someone else. They are taught from a young age to go to school and get good grades in order to get accepted into a good college or university. Colleges, in turn, teach students how to sell themselves to large corporations in order to get a good job with a decent salary. In this situation, new employees are often satisfied, but this is when they step into a trap. The problem is that most people don't even realize that they are in a trap until they realize that their jobs control their time, money, and lives. More importantly, their jobs control their destiny. This is because the reason they have worked so hard for is now the thing that holds them back. People find that they have worked hard and made increasingly more money and may have even received a promotion that gives them more money and more responsibility.

What does the average employee do with a raise? For most people, a raise causes them to want more and, in return, spend more. Along comes the purchase of a bigger house in a nicer neighborhood with better schools and a new car, all while getting deeper into debt. Before long one of the children is heading off to college and people begin to wonder why they work so hard. Is it to survive, or to have a few of life's luxuries? Let me tell you from my own experience that life does not have to be this way. You can have all the wealth and time you want by changing your habits and the way you think. After reading this book, you will not only have gained knowledge but you will know how to put that knowledge to use in order to succeed.

The problem of working for other people is that most companies have a management structure shaped like a pyramid. New employees start at the bottom of the pyramid, and near the top are the higher paid managers. As employees work their way up to the top of the pyramid it narrows to a point and it becomes obvious that only a handful of employees are going to be able to move into the top positions.

Do you agree with the following statement?: "We all know that when a promotional position opens up in a company the best candidate is selected to fill the position." If you agree with this statement, you're living in a perfect world and should immediately give this book to someone who needs it. If you disagree, you are like the vast majority of the employees, who complain that favoritism plays a key role in promotions at their place of employment.

> *"If your job is your only opportunity for financial gain, you're setting yourself up for disappointment."*

This is not even the worst that goes on in the work place. Have you ever heard the saying "He who works the hardest gets all the work" or, "No good deed goes unpunished"? You need to know that there is some truth to these statements. There is plenty of information out there about unfair workplaces, but what can you do? Before we get to that, let's take another look at your employer and what he controls.

No matter how hard you work, your employer controls your finances by putting a cap on how much you can earn. Your supervisor is in control of whether you will get a promotion, and controls your time by telling you when to work and for how long. Your employer controls your destiny by deciding how far you will move up the ladder and when. The reality is that your employer not only controls your income, your time, and your destiny but also, ultimately, controls your life. The time has come for you to take back your life and to be in charge of your own future. This will, of course, take time and hard work; however, the rewards will be far greater than what you might imagine.

We live in a country where great opportunity knocks at your door waiting to be opened. Don't ignore the knocking or the ghost of opportunity may never return. Just remember that the excuse of waiting for the right time comes out of fear and procrastination. Start right now and tell yourself that you control your life and your destiny.

"All of your actions are either positive or negative."

The reason I wrote this book is to give people a guide that addresses the desire and need to make one's life better, both financially and spiritually. Most ambitious people have pondered their lives at some point and find themselves wanting something more but perhaps don't know where to start. Reading this book will help you get answers to your questions about changing your life, and at the very least you will have the knowledge to get started in the process of change and learn what to do when opportunities present themselves.

Before we get started, let's be realistic. Almost everyone has seen and heard about get-rich-quick schemes that sound good, look good, and seem to work. People initially tell themselves that they can succeed in such programs, but then realize what is involved: too much time, too much money, and too much sweat equity. For instance, some of the real estate courses I've encountered tell students to look at 100 homes being sold by motivated sellers; the program's system works through the process of elimination.

Considering that today's average household consists of two parents who work full-time and are juggling to raise two or three children, who has the time to look at 100 homes? Most parents can't find the time to have their teeth cleaned. So, the search goes on. People continue to look for that one opportunity to improve their financial status without having to quit their jobs or disrupt their family's balance, but the better life and financial freedom infomercials speak of are not available to the average household. Who has the time to do what they request of people? The next time you're watching such an advertisement, ask yourself, "What do they do with their children?" or, "Am I willing to quit my job to take a chance at this?"

At this point in your life, you more than likely view time as your biggest enemy, but in reality it can be your best friend. In this book, I will teach you how to get the most out of your time and, by using that extra time, increase your personal wealth. Through it all you should keep in mind that wealth takes time and time builds wealth, two things infomercials and get-rich-quick schemes rarely take the time to emphasize.

2

Improving Your Credit

The first step in becoming financially independent is to understand the difference between assets and liabilities. Chances are that most of the people you know and work with have far more liabilities than assets, which is why they are working to pay off their debts.

In this chapter I will show you several ways to decrease your liabilities and, as result, how to have a higher monthly cash flow. In turn, this will allow you to purchase assets that will give you additional cash flow.

Stop. Go back and carefully reread the last sentence of the previous paragraph so you fully understand its meaning. Whether you believe it or not, that one sentence holds your key to wealth. Once you understand that the more assets you purchase the more wealth you will obtain and the more cash flow you have the more you can purchase, you will see how the process continues to repeat itself. It is, of course, up to you to get it started.

That being said, let's learn the difference between assets and liabilities by starting with the definition of an asset. Assets are anything that put money in your pocket such as jobs, rental real estate, stocks, and royalties. Generally speaking your house isn't an asset, and I will explain why when we get to liabilities.

Except for your job, you may find that you don't have any assets that provide you with cash flow; however, there is what I call secondary assets that you own and will give you cash when you sell them (such as antiques, coins, stamps, cars, etc.). These items don't cost you anything to own, but they do have value and could be sold if necessary.

Liabilities, on the other hand, are any items that take money out of your pocket such as car loans, credit card debt, utilities, or mortgages. As I mentioned before, the home in which you live in is a liability for several reasons. First, since you will always need a place to live, your primary residence will continually cost you money. Second, even if your primary residence is paid for, you must pay property taxes as a part of ownership. In reality, the home in which you live will always cost you money, which means it will always be a liability. However, you can use your ownership in a home to your financial advantage. First, owning a home allows you to build the equity that accompanies appreciation; you can't build equity if you are a renter. Second, homeowners can use their equity to get a line of credit

(LOC), discussed in Chapter 6, or as collateral to secure short-term loans. Homeowners should not use home equity loans to pay off their debts. In Chapter 6, "Making the Purchase," I will show you a far better use for the equity in your home if your goal is to make money.

The first step toward becoming financially independent is to come up with a plan to decrease your liabilities (debt). Part of that plan is to limit the amount of cash you carry with you, since it's been proven that the more cash you carry the more apt you are to spend it. You can make it a game to see how long the cash in your pocket can last, and this will help teach you discipline when it comes to saving money.

> ### *"A key to wealth is to buy assets to pay for your liabilities."*

At the beginning of the week give yourself a certain amount of cash to carry. Your goal is to keep the cash as long as possible without spending it. The following week, see how much you have left from the week before and decrease the amount you take from your paycheck. Every week decrease the amount of cash you carry until you find your balance and stick with it. I know you are thinking that it's going to take a lot more than saving a little bit of cash each week; however, the purpose of this exercise is to change your habits from spending to saving. You will be surprised at how much you can save if you make it your goal and write it down. A key element to financial freedom is having good habits when it comes to money management. When you accomplish the task of saving instead of spending it sets your mind frame to save on an even larger scale. It will also help to write down what you spend your money on. At the end of the week evaluate the list and make necessary changes to increase your savings even further.

> ***"You have to tighten up your financial belt today to bring you wealth tomorrow."***

The next exercise is for you to take all of your credit cards, place them in a box, pick two to keep, and cut up the rest. Take the statements on the credit cards that you cut up and close the accounts that have zero balances. The fewer credit card accounts you have open the higher your credit score will be; even if you have credit cards with zero balances they still have an adverse effect on your credit score. Unless you pay off your balance every month, it's very important to limit the use of your credit cards. Since you want to keep your debt ratio as low as possible, you must pay off your remaining credit card balances. Devise a plan to pay off one credit card at a time by starting with the one that has the highest interest rate and paying the minimum on the others. One by one you will pay them off and close the account of cards you will not keep.

You must also understand that there are two types of debt: good debt and bad debt. Good debt is, obviously, the kind you want: debt that gives you cash flow, such as real estate. You don't want bad debt, which takes money out of your pocket, such as car payments, credit card debt, luxury items, and expenses.

"It is not how much you earn, it's how much you save."

Up to this point if you have agreed to do what you have been asked to do, you are well on your way to financial freedom. Speaking of financial freedom, have you noticed that every successful company, corporation, and even the government makes a budget to manage spending? The reason for this is to keep spending in check and stay out of the red. Obviously, the government spends a lot of time in the red; however, the government will never go bankrupt thanks to taxpayers. Try asking your boss for an advance on your paycheck to cover your overdue bill; chances are he will either laugh in your face or look at you like you're crazy.

Becoming financially responsible is another key to financial freedom. Let's face it: nobody is going to bail us out when we get into financial trouble, and so making a budget is far more important to your financial success than you had perhaps ever realized unless, of course, you have an endless supply of money or a wealthy uncle who really likes you.

In order to make a budget that works, you will have to write down all of your monthly expenses such as food, utilities (gas, electric, cable, etc...), and gasoline for your automobiles. List them all and – most important – be honest about what you pay every month. Take the total and divide it by two if you are paid bi-weekly (every other week). This is how much you will pay for food, utilities, and gasoline per paycheck. I left out your mortgage (or rent) and auto payments because they are a monthly expense due the same time every month and thus rather difficult to divide into payments twice a month. As an alternative, for example, if your car payment is due on the 18th of the month, you would budget the payment on your paycheck you receive the week before the car payment is due (see example below):

July 10, 2005

$ 800.00	Carry over from last pay date
+ 1,000.00	Paycheck
1,800.00	**Balance**
- 400.00	Food, utilities, gas (F.U.G)
1,400.00	**Subtotal**
- 400.00	Car payment
1,000.00	**Subtotal**
- 300.00	Spending money
$ 700.00	**Carry over to next pay date**

July 24, 2005

$ 700.00	Carry over from last pay date
+ 1,000.00	Paycheck
1,700.00	**Balance**
- 400.00	Food, utilities, gas [F.U.G]
1,300.00	**Subtotal**
- 800.00	Mortgage
500.00	**Subtotal**
- 200.00	Spending money
$ 300.00	**Carry over to next pay date**

Don't forget to keep a little bit of your paycheck for spending money (fun money). This will also help give you a cushion if you fall short or if something unexpected comes up. Also remember to put money in to a savings account and, if you can, have a certain amount directly deposited into savings. This is what the wealthy commonly refer to as "paying yourself first." The money from your savings account will give you the opportunity to invest at a later time. If you don't use direct deposit, make it a habit to deposit a set amount of money into your savings account every paycheck and include it on your budget if you think you might forget.

In time this money will pave your way to financial freedom. I suggest that you sit down and create a budget that is good for the next three months and remember to break your bills (liabilities) down to the days on which you are paid on. Your goal with budgeting is to save for future investments that will provide you with cash flow. The more you save, the sooner you can start bringing in cash flow.

If you're an average person you have a car loan; next to paying for housing, a car loan is the second largest liability you have. If you are in this situation, which many people are, you need to pay off your car loan in a timely manner and keep driving that car until it falls apart. The reason for this is that you don't want to tie up more of your hard-earned income on a new car (new liability) because it will only set you back financially. As for your mortgage, it is necessary to have a place to live. The best path to take here is not to buy a house larger or more expensive than what you need. If you are renting, you will be better off financially to purchase your own home. If they are all that you can afford, condominiums, town homes, or small ranches are all better than paying rent. At the very least you will be building appreciation on the liability (your home) and will have more tax benefits at the end of the year.

"You should review your bank statements for errors."

Let me repeat something I said before. One of the key elements to financial freedom is having good habits. You are probably asking yourself what good habits I'm talking about. What I'm referring to are organization, goal setting, planning, and being open minded. It is important that you incorporate these habits into your daily routine in order to improve your life. I have listed these habits below along with the meaning of each. After reading over the list, you may find the tasks involved to be simple. The point here is for you to practice the habits so they become routine, and as time goes on you will learn to challenge yourself with more difficult tasks.

Organization

Organizational skills top the list of good habits of successful people. It's almost impossible to be successful without being organized. Disorganized people are the ones who can't seem to find what they are looking for, which causes them to waste valuable time looking for what they can't find. These people are often late to appointments and miss opportunities that are right in front of them. Organizational skills are an easy habit to maintain with practice, starting at home. Walk through your house room by room and make a list of what you have to organize. Set a date by which you will have organized each room, and stick to your schedule. It is important that you stay on your time line because it will develop an "I will get it done" attitude. Buy organizers to separate your belongings and don't be afraid to throw things away. While you are organizing each room, don't forget to set up an area to keep all of your bills and important papers. Purchase file folders and paper-bins to place your bills in. If you need ideas on how to organize paperwork and bills go to an office supply store in your area and ask for advice in finding the right supplies.

"Use your free time wisely"

Goal Setting

In the beginning, set goals you know you can accomplish. This will help motivate you. When you set goals write them down along with the date by which you want to have them completed. This habit will re-enforce the importance of getting it done. When you have achieved each goal, cross it off your list. This will also help motivate you to move on to the next goal. Setting a goal can be as simple as washing your car or cleaning your basement. Don't overload yourself with goals to the point where you have too much anxiety about getting things done. The important thing to remember at this point is that goal setting and organizational skills go hand and hand with success.

Planning

After you set your goals you will need a plan on how to accomplish them. Plans should be detailed in a series of small steps to show what needs to be done from start to finish. As you complete each step, cross it off your list. This will give you a sense of accomplishment as well as motivate you to complete your goal.

Being Open Minded

Get in the habit of keeping your mind open to possibilities. This habit is the foundation of a positive attitude. Never think "I can't do that." Instead, ask yourself, "How can I do that?" Keeping an open mind will allow you to absorb more opportunities than you have in the past. Rather than doubting yourself, expand your horizons.

Notes

3

Investing in Real Estate

You may be asking yourself what a good long-term investment might be. My answer is simple: real estate. If you're wondering why, there are far more reasons than I could even give you in one book; however, in this chapter I will outline the main reasons why you should invest in real estate if you're looking for a stable long-term way to earn money.

First, if done properly, you will be financially free within five to ten years. You may be wondering what "financial freedom" is; I define it as being able to live well on the passive income derived from real estate. This depends, of course, on your desire to learn and your ambition to get ahead by sticking to your goals. The more real estate you purchase, the larger your financial base will be, and with a larger financial base you will find more opportunities that you can take action on. Correctly done, all of the real estate you purchase will give you monthly cash flow. That's right: cash flow. Multiply your monthly cash flow per unit by the number of units owned, and you will come up with what real estate investors refer to as passive income. Passive income is income from a source you don't have to work at every day. For instance, the most common forms of passive income are real estate rentals, royalties, and business ownership. Passive income is the least taxed income you can have.

Imagine owning a property with a mortgage of $1,200 a month. The principal and interest are $900, taxes are $200, insurance is $50, and mortgage insurance (PMI) is $50 a month. In this situation, you could realistically have a tenant paying $1,500 a month in rent, leaving you not only with your tenant paying your mortgage but with an additional tax write off of $1,200, plus a $300 positive monthly cash flow.

Now at this point you may be thinking that either this only exist in a perfect world or that you don't feel comfortable dealing with tenants. You are right that we don't live in a perfect world in which everyone does what is right, which can affect your relationship with potential and current tenants; however, in Chapters 7 and 8, I will teach you techniques to eliminate 95 percent of tenant problems. Through it all, just remember to listen to your own instincts and don't worry about other people's opinions, unless they are objective and come from someone truly trying to help you. Some of the richest people in the world listen to their inner desires and use their passions to accomplish what they want. You must build this same positive attitude; with it you will accomplish what others tell you cannot be done.

I admit that there is risk involved. If you are logical and think objectively you realize there is risk in almost everything you do. Financially savvy people find ways to limit their exposure to that risk, and I will show you why real estate has the least amount of risk but the largest potential for reward. Real estate is far more stable than any other investment, which is an important factor to keep in mind when deciding what path you want to take to build – and keep – your wealth.

> ***"The appreciation for real estate over the past 30 years has averaged more than 6 percent."***

Most of you reading this book are employees working for a paycheck. It is important to remember that a large percentage of retirement plans are invested in the stock market in one way or another, which puts the fate of your retirement fund in the hands of other people, for better or for worse. Real estate, on the other hand, has its own track record. When you take a look at real estate it does not matter whether interest rates are high or low; you can still make a profit. It's all about finding the right deal. The better the deal, the less risk involved with a larger chance to profit. Try that with the stock market! Another drawback to being an employee is that your salary is usually your only income. Believe it or not, you put yourself at a higher risk of financial failure relying solely on earned income than you would by producing passive income.

Let's say that as an employee you are injured and cannot work for a period of time. Even if you have temporary disability insurance, you will lose at least some of your income because in order to get paid in full you must show up for work. Your retirement fund is also going to suffer because, unless you're getting a paycheck there is no money being saved. You also might even need to borrow from your retirement plan to make ends meet. This highlights one of the many negatives of making a living solely from earned income: You're always at the mercy of your employer or other circumstances which are largely beyond your control.

The benefit of passive income is that you can be passive and still get paid. You can collect rent, even if you are injured. In extreme circumstances where you are incapacitated further, you can hire people to handle affairs that you can not, a step most professional investors do anyway to save time.

Types of Real Estate Investors

Let's examine the basic types of real estate investors. Depending on where you live there may be different terms or definitions.

Landlords

Landlords are technically investors. They are people who purchase real estate for the sole purpose of renting it out to tenants. Most landlords have a handful of properties, usually residential rentals. When repairs or maintenance are necessary a landlord normally handles it himself. Landlords usually keep their rental properties for longer periods of time. Most landlords lack the necessary insurance or business structure to protect themselves from rental losses and liability lawsuits.

Professional Investors

Professional investors are people or companies who purchase a variety of different types of real estate for the purpose of generating cash flow and appreciation. The real estate they purchase may be residential, commercial, industrial, or land properties. These investors are constantly re-evaluating the properties they own for the possibility of selling because doing so creates new opportunities to purchase larger properties with the expectation of a further increase in cash flow. Most of the property professional investors purchase is only owned for a short time, often between four to seven years. Investors may also use management companies to handle the day-to-day responsibilities of ownership, which, frees up time to search for more property to purchase. Professional investors usually hold their real estate investment properties under some form of business structure.

Hard Money Investors

Hard money investors are people who put up money to assist in the purchase of real estate for a return on their money. Where a landlord owns his property and is responsible for its overall control and decision making regarding the property, hard money investors lend their money to a purchaser or developer to later collect a certain pre-agreed return on their money. Since hard money investors enter into real estate deals strictly for short-term monetary benefit and only work with people they know to be successful, he or she will rarely have anything to do with day-to-day operations. In order to be this type of investor you must either have cash on hand or access to quick cash. I strongly advise that you have a lot of experience before going into any business venture of this sort.

From this point on, when I use the word 'investor' I will be referring to landlords; however, your personal goal should be to become a professional investor.

Flipping Property

Because the subject of flipping properties could be a book all by itself, I will only touch on the subject. The basic premise behind flipping property is to buy a property for a low price, fix it up, and then sell it for a profit. For example, a person wanting to flip a property would look to purchase one being or that could be sold well under the market value. There are many reasons for a property to be sold under the market value such as foreclosure, divorce, retirement, death, major repairs, or the owner being anxious to sell.

The key is to find a motivated seller who wants a quick sale. You can purchase the property; bring it up to the standard of other houses in the area, then sell it at market value to a new owner and move on to the next property. Each time you flip a property you can refine your system to better suit your needs. Keep in mind that this example is very brief and seems to be simple; nonetheless, I assure you that flipping property takes knowledge, persistence, and at least a little bit of money.

Since you must be on your toes throughout the entire process of flipping a property, it's not for you if you are a procrastinator. While being good at flipping property has the potential to make you very wealthy, it does take hard work, research, and knowledge. You will need to know the market and how to turn a profit in a timely manner. Since the rental market is far more forgiving of mistakes than the process of flipping properties, most investors get their feet wet with residential rentals.

Unless you have a lot of extra cash on hand (which most people don't), experience in real estate is always helpful if you are looking to flip property. This is why I suggest starting with residential rentals, since they will give you an understanding of what is involved in real estate transactions and offer you the opportunity to build up your financial base and cash reserves.

Types of Rentals

There are three common types of rental property: residential, commercial, and industrial. While I will touch on commercial and industrial properties so you can understand they are an option once your base of knowledge expands, I will primarily focus on residential rentals. Commercial rental markets tend to be more risky, but can also be highly profitable if handled correctly.

Residential rentals are by far the most common real estate investment. Residential housing includes single family homes, townhomes, condominiums, and multi-family buildings. Single family homes come in two different types: detached (the most common) and attached. Detached, or stand alone, homes occupy a single lot and are not attached to any other structure, whereas attached homes – also known as townhomes, duplexes, or condominiums, share at least one common wall with another home. There are pros and cons to purchasing and renting each of the different types of houses offered on the market. With my explanations below, you will find an abundance of variety available to give you an idea of what type of investment to start searching for.

Houses (detached)

Detached homes are the most common type sold on the real estate market. These types of homes are usually two-story or ranch style houses with yards.

The benefits of owning this type of house is that it stands alone and has a yard, which means owners don't have to deal with neighbors sharing a common wall or walkway. This means there will be less noise for your tenants, and these homes usually have a higher resale value.

The down side of owning a detached home is that you become solely responsible for all of the repairs and maintenance of the house. Unless you make other arrangements, you will have to cut the grass and shovel the snow. When renting out a home, you should be aware that it is difficult to keep up with the exterior of the home without the cooperation of your tenants.

Townhouses, Condominiums, and Lofts (attached)

Attached homes include townhouses, condominiums, and lofts. In some states a townhouse is considered to be a condominium. Townhouses are usually built side-by-side in a two-story building with up to eight units attached to each other. Condominiums (condos) and lofts are normally built like apartment buildings and units are sold individually.

The benefit of owning a townhome is that they are easier to maintain since most of them are part of a Homeowners Association (HOA) that is responsible for maintaining the building's exterior and common areas. These areas usually include the roof, siding, windows, walkways, driveways, and landscaping. For example, homeowners associations cut the grass and clear the snow from walks and driveway. As far as the resale market is concerned, townhomes are rather easy to sell since they target first-time home buyers and empty-nesters looking to downsize their space.

The down side of owning attached units is that some homeowners associations have expensive monthly fees and may also have strict rules on rentals. Some HOAs have even prohibited the leasing of any unit under their control. Also, because attached units share at least one common wall with other homes, you may experience problems with an adjacent unit if there is a fire or water leak.

Multi-Family Homes

A multi-family home is any building consisting of two or more units, including duplexes (two units), two-flats, and apartment buildings.

The benefit of multi-family homes is that you can have a lot of rental units in one location, which means your profit margin is usually larger.

Apartments are easy to rent out if they are well kept.

The down side of these homes is that you are responsible for all of the maintenance and repairs, including landscaping, grass cutting, snow removal, and upkeep of common areas. As with attached housing, any damage caused to one unit may result in damage to several other units. Tenant problems can also be a concern, but the majority of issues concerning tenants can be kept to a minimum by having a well written lease, a good screening process, and a well maintained property. These subjects will be covered in detail in Chapter 7.

Be aware that in the beginning of your real estate investment career you will want to keep your expenses down. Newer properties will have fewer problems than older properties, and recently built units are more likely to be up to current code and building regulations.

Don't be afraid of properties with Homeowners Associations (HOA), but make sure that before you put a purchase contract on a property with a HOA you find out what the monthly fee is going to be in order to make sure it will be financially viable. Your projected profit margin will determine whether you continue with the purchase. Be sure to put a clause in the purchase contract that stipulates that you must have an updated copy of the HOA rules and regulations from the seller and that the sale is contingent upon the HOA allowing the owners to rent out their units. The last thing you want to happen is to purchase a property only to find out when it's too late that you can't rent it out. Most

HOAs will let you rent out the unit, as long as you agree to be ultimately responsible for the property and its upkeep. Most HOAs will also stipulate that leases must be no less than one year long. Know the HOA's rules and regulations before you purchase or it may end up being a very expensive learning experience.

4

Getting Started

This chapter will walk you through the basic steps to become a successful real estate investor. Take the following recommendations seriously and try to accomplish as many of them as possible, since when you do it right the first time you will have better opportunities and fewer setbacks in the future.

Post Office Box (P.O. Box)

One of the first orders of business is to establish a post office box, which is a numbered mailbox with a lock located at your local post office. There are several different sizes available to rent on an annual or semi-annual basis. The rental cost is determined by the size of the box and is fairly inexpensive. Beside the fact that you will not want your tenants to have your home address, having a post office box address looks far more professional.

Checking Account

Establish a checking account for your properties. This will be your operating fund for your mortgages, bills, repairs, and maintenance. Although it's fine to have a personal savings account to save money to be used as a down payment to purchase investment properties, do not mix your personal money with your business money. Your business checking account should have a minimum of three months of mortgage payments per property owned as cash reserves. Unless prohibited by law, it's a good idea to keep your tenants' security deposits in this account. Make sure to check with state and local government agencies for the requirements on proper handling of security deposits. Some may require you to keep security deposits in a separate interest-bearing account with the interest being paid to the tenants upon the end of the lease.

"Don't forget to keep your business of real estate separate from your personal bank accounts and bills."

Lines of Credit (LOC)

A line of credit can be useful if you run into unexpected expenses. Depending on your credit rating, your bank may be willing to give you a small line of credit without putting up any collateral; however, most banks will request some type of collateral such as home equity, an automobile, bonds, a certificate of deposit (CD), or a savings account. Of course, most banks prefer home equity. Check with your local banks to see what programs they offer. Remember that this line of credit is for emergencies only and not to be used as a down payment for a property. The line of credit you apply for should be just enough that you feel comfortable with. In Chapter 6, "Making the Purchase" I will explain how to use your equity to cash out on a refinance.

Understanding Your Credit Report

Buying a property is much easier with a good credit score. Your credit report shows your record of debt repayment and lists any bankruptcy filings, judgments, foreclosures, liens, or civil suits. A credit report is obtained from your creditors notifying one or all three credit reporting bureaus (Equifax, Trans Union, and Experian /TRW) about your repayment history. The credit bureaus do not accept or reject applications for credit, nor do they give an overall rating of an individual's credit report. Creditors with whom you apply for credit are prohibited from supplying you with a copy of any credit report, including your own; if you want a copy you must request it from one of the three reporting bureaus. In order to dispute information on your credit report you must do it in writing, at which point the credit reporting bureau will contact the creditor who provided the disputed information. If the bureau cannot confirm the information it will be removed from your credit report.

Your overall credit score will be negatively affected every time you apply for a loan or a credit card. This will show as an "inquiry" on your credit report. Even if they have zero balances, open credit cards listed on your credit report cause your score to drop. In order to increase your credit score you must keep a minimum number of credit cards and pay down your debt. This is why it's important to follow the steps in Chapter 2 to help you reduce your debt.

Credit Bureaus

Equifax – *www.equifax.com*
To order your report, call: 800-685-1111
To report fraud, call: 800-525-6285
TDD 800-255-0056
Address: P.O. Box 740241, Atlanta, GA.
      30374-0241

Experian – *www.experia.com*
To order your report, call: 888-397-3742
To report fraud, call: 888-397-3742
TDD 800-972-0322
Address: P.O. Box 9532, Allen, TX. 75013

TransUnion – *www.transunion.com*
To order your report, call: 800-888-4213
To report fraud, call: 800-680-7289
TDD 877-553-7803
Address: P.O. Box 6790, Fullerton, CA.
92834-6790

Pay Yourself First

Save money from every paycheck and place it into a savings account. If you do this consistently, your savings can build quickly, and having cash on hand will allow you to take advantage of new investment opportunities. When you are able to rent out properties, or when you sell them, you will start making money and have a positive cash flow.

*"The key is to save
so you can buy."*

Minding Your Own Business

In order to mind your own business you must gain knowledge that makes you an expert in your field. Go to real estate seminars and classes. The more research you do the more you will learn. Don't ever stop learning what is new in real estate. If you have a question, search for the answer. If you have a problem, find the solution.

Don't ever stop learning because if you do you have closed your mind to new ideas and new opportunities. Start small and dream big, for one day the world will be yours. Check the "Resource List" at the end of this book for recommended reading.

> ## *"You don't need a degree to invest in real estate, it can be learned."*

Networking

Connecting with other real estate investors will improve your knowledge and skills. Find a local real estate investor's club or start one up on your own. There are several resources you can use to find active clubs such as newspapers, telephone books, and the Internet. Being a member of an investor's organization will not only improve your knowledge, it will also help you get useful information on written forms (e.g., leases and contracts), laws, and business contacts.

> ## *"Don't forget to check the Internet for landlord associations."*

Professional investors are glad to share this type of information with you, and some may even help you with the purchase because they know there are plenty of deals out there for all of you. Having this type of support will prove to be invaluable to your future success.

Notes

5

Building Your Team

To be a successful real estate investor you don't have to know everything about real estate, but it is necessary to have a team of knowledgeable professionals to assist you. I have compiled a list of professionals you should have on your team. Keep in mind that you will only pay for their services when you use them.

Real Estate Agents

I like to use at least two real estate agents from different realtors. When I search for a new agent I tell them I am an investor and want to speak with the person who handles investment properties. Most offices have at least one realtor who handles investors, if they don't keep searching.

Mortgage Broker/Banker

Find a mortgage broker who caters to investors. Mortgage brokers are usually better than mortgage bankers for several reasons. First, brokers are working for you and only get paid if you get a loan. The banker works for the bank and it is his job to protect the bank's assets. A good broker can coach you on how to get approved for a loan, which can save you a lot of potential trouble. Developing a long-term relationship with a broker will make it easier to get mortgages because he or she will understand what you are trying to accomplish and will have all your information on file. When you need a pre-approval letter for a property deal, your broker can quickly provide you with one. Mortgage brokers deal with lenders who usually have very structured loan criteria. Lenders who use mortgage brokers will more than likely sell your mortgage to another larger lender. Even though mortgage brokers work for you and mortgage bankers work for the bank, don't count bankers out completely because many of them can change loan criteria to fit your needs in certain circumstances. Unless you have a mortgage banker with whom you are comfortable, my advice is to use a mortgage broker for your first few purchases.

Real Estate Attorney

You will need a real estate attorney. Make sure to get one who handles a lot of real estate transactions. While you will mostly need your attorney for contract review and closings, it's definitely a plus if he or she has experience dealing with tenant issues (such as evictions). Don't be apprehensive about changing lawyers if one of them doesn't meet your expectations.

Home Inspector

While some people might think home inspections are optional, money spent on home inspectors is money well spent. Not only can home inspectors potentially save you thousands of dollars in hidden damages and code violations, they will give you peace of mind with your purchase.

> *"Multifamily homes and commercial properties cost more to inspect than single family homes."*

Insurance Agent

In the real estate business insurance is a necessity. Most, if not all, lenders will require you to have insurance. You will also want to purchase an umbrella policy to cover all of your insured property, including your residence, investment property, business, and automobiles. Umbrella policies are fairly inexpensive for the amount of protection they offer, not to mention the peace of mind, since an umbrella policy will cover you if you are found to be liable in a lawsuit.

For instance, let's say that one of your tenants tells you the carpet on the steps leading to his apartment is loose. Three weeks later you find out the tenant is suing you because he fell down the same steps and broke his leg. His lawyers take you to court for monetary damages and his loss of pay while out of work. The court agrees with the tenant's lawyers under the premise that you should have repaired the steps sooner and you are therefore found liable for damages to the tenant. If your insurance policy for that property does not cover the total cost of damages due, your umbrella policy will kick in and cover the outstanding balance. If you do not have an umbrella policy then you will be personally responsible for the outstanding balance.

You can also protect yourself personally by placing the property under a Limited Liability Company (LLC) or Limited Partnership (LP). I will explain these options in Chapter 9, "Protecting Your Investment with an LLC."

Landlord Policy

For your investment properties, do not just get a regular run of the mill insurance policy. Since you want to protect yourself from lawsuits and disasters, residential rental property requires a specialized policy, such as a landlord protection plan or a real estate rental policy.

The most common disaster you may deal with is fire. Let's say you own a two-story, four-unit building in which the upstairs tenant has a stove fire that damages the kitchen. While putting out the fire, the local fire department causes water damage to the downstairs apartment and, until the damage is repaired, both of the apartments will be uninhabitable. If the estimated time for the repairs to be completed is four months, you (as the landlord) have two problems. First, your tenants must live somewhere else for the next four months, which means you won't be collecting rent on those two apartments. Second, your mortgage lender will expect you to continue to pay your mortgage and taxes. You need to protect yourself against such unexpected disasters or you can lose large amounts of money.

The extra cost of a landlord protection plan is worth it for several reasons. First, as in the scenario above, your rents are covered. Second, since your insurance company is paying lost rental income while repairs are being completed, the insurance company will ensure that they are completed in a timely manner. After all, the insurance company doesn't want to put out any more money than necessary. Get the proper insurance coverage so you don't have any setbacks that will slow down your progress in building your financial future.

When choosing an insurance agent, request information about the policies his or her company offers. If the agent does not appear to be knowledgeable on the subjects you're concerned about, you may be better off going elsewhere. Don't stop looking until you find an agent who is knowledgeable and with whom you feel comfortable working with.

Tax Accountant

Don't even think about leaving this person off your team. Since tax laws are complicated and constantly changing, most professional investors have tax accountants. Find a tax accountant who is experienced in real estate. When it is time to pay your taxes, an accountant becomes extremely valuable and he or she will help you make far more money then you will ever pay them. Your accountant will also be valuable to you during the off-season and can keep your financial accounts in order if necessary. As your investments grow you will need the assistance of an accountant more and more.

Credit Checks

When you start screening prospective tenants you should always run credit checks and charge prospective tenants an application fee to cover your costs. There are numerous companies that offer special packages and pricing for investors. Since some real estate investor groups or landlord associations have discounted packages with certain vendors, it may be beneficial for you to become a member of one or more of these associations. Check the "Resource List" at the end of the book for a listing of recommended Web sites.

Debt Collections

Unfortunately, in the real estate rental business you may have to undertake the unpleasant task of evicting a tenant. The majority of evictions are a result of the failure to pay rent. While you can often easily obtain a court judgment for lost rent, attorney fees, court fees, and damages, you may have a difficult time recovering the amount awarded to you. This is why I recommend finding a professional debt collection company to pursue the collection of your judgment. Most companies will assign one person to handle your case and will have you transfer the court judgment over to them before they will attempt any method of collection. Even though the usual customary fee is 40 to 50 percent of any money recovered, remember that half of the money is better than no money. In addition to helping you ensure you will get the money owed to you, retaining a professional collection company sets an example for your other tenants that you operate as a professional real estate investor.

In order to collect debts professional collection companies have resources available to them that you may not, such as wage garnishment, credit reporting, seizure of bank accounts, or seizure of property. Of course this would have to be by court order, but the companies will do all the work for you. Most states have laws allowing interest charges to be added on to any unpaid balance of a court judgment; check with your state or county government for details. Your collection company should also have knowledge of any laws pertaining to this subject.

6

Making the Purchase

In this chapter I will walk you through the purchase process so you will have a worry-free closing and discuss step by step what is necessary to make a successful purchase. First, you must start by letting other people know you're an investor looking for real estate property. Get business cards stating that you are a real estate investor and add a statement to them that you will pay a finders fee to any person who directs you to a property you end up purchasing. Notify your real estate agents that you are looking for investment properties, making sure that you elaborate upon what type of property you are willing to purchase.

Don't forget to look in the local newspapers and online for advertisements. You want to find properties that mostly need minor and cosmetic repairs. Be patient and the right opportunity will present itself.

Numbers on Paper

Make sure you work out the numbers on paper before you place a purchase contract on any property. The property must have a positive cash flow when you buy it. Let's say you're looking at a townhome priced at $170,000. Obviously, you are not going to pay the asking price; therefore, you decide to make a $150,000 offer. (Remember that the price of real estate is determined by how much you want it. Don't let anyone tell you you're bidding too low; the seller makes that decision. This is why it's good to find motivated sellers.) The townhome has three bedrooms and two baths and is located in an excellent school district. The market rent in the area for that type of property is approximately $1,500 per month. Assuming your tenants will pay utilities, your numbers would look like this:

Principle & Interest (mortgage) $ 900
Taxes.....................................200
Hazard Insurance 40
Homeowners Association 70
PMI (Lender's Insurance)..............90
Total monthly payment $1,300

In this situation, the rent collected is $1,500 and your expenses for the property (total monthly payment) are $1,300. This means your cash flow will be $200. Make sure you set a minimum limit on cash flow per month. Because there may be unexpected changes or shortfalls when you close on a property, it is better to set the cash flow higher than what you're looking for. You will always want to have a cushion on paper in case your figures are a little off. Do not get emotionally attached to any property you look at. It is just business. The numbers must work on paper with a cash flow cushion. If they don't, drop the property and move on to the next one. This way you will establish a fail-safe system based on financial intelligence, not gut feelings. To ensure your success, stick to your set standard for monthly cash flow per property. Since every part of the country is different, I cannot tell you what your minimum cash flow should be. Just remember to be realistic. The more experience you gain the more proficient you will become at fine-tuning this process.

"Have at least three
months of cash reserves."

What to Consider

When searching for the right investment property you will have to consider what you want. For instance, how many bedrooms, baths, or fireplaces? Do you want a basement or a slab foundation? For a number of reasons, I stay away from fireplaces and basements in my rental units. Do you really want tenants starting fires in your rental units? Because of the added risk and liability of fire and/or injury (especially to children) I certainly don't. You also have to consider the cost of maintenance and the possibility of smoke damage with fireplaces. A high-end rental unit may be fine with a fireplace; however, I would not recommend it in the average rental unit.

Basements are another area of concern. While basements offer tenants more room, you need to consider the possibilities of flooding, animal infestations, and the question of a tenant's personal property being stored in the basement. You must also take into consideration that a large number of prospective tenants have children and pets. As you know they both can cause more accidental damage to a wooden sub-floor (present in homes with basements) than a slab of concrete. Even though you will have to weigh the positives and negatives carefully, the best way to avoid problems with liabilities and damage is to avoid the problems in the first place.

The Purchase

Once you have chosen a financially viable investment property, you will be ready to make an offer. Whether you find this property through a real estate agent or on your own you will need a purchase contract to make an offer. A real estate agent will supply a basic contract used for the area where the property is located. If you're the one who found the property and a real estate agent is being used you will have several options in order to obtain a copy of a purchase contract.

"Don't sacrifice cash flow for appreciation."

First, if you have a real estate agent on your team, ask him or her for a blank copy of a real estate purchase contract. If your agent knows you are a repeat customer, he or she will usually be happy to supply you with whatever you need. Second, your attorney should have a blank copy of a real estate purchase contract. Third, you can purchase one at an office supply store. In this case, I recommend reading it carefully or, better yet, having your attorney review it. Fourth, you can make a contract up yourself. Unless you have strong experience with these types of contracts and transactions, I strongly discourage this. Fifth, you could join a club or association for landlords, either locally or on the Internet. Not only will such associations be able to provide you with contracts, they will also have other helpful resources. (See the "Resource List" at the end of the book for information on landlord association Web sites.)

Once you have obtained a blank copy of the proper real estate purchase contract you will be ready to fill in the information. When using a real estate agent he or she will fill out the purchase contract for your approval. In order to protect yourself as an investor, there are a few conditions you will want to add to all real estate purchase contracts. First, insert a line stating, "This offer is contingent upon the approval of my partner." Your partner can be anybody or nobody. It doesn't matter who your "partner" is or if you even have a partner. The reason you will put this in is that it will give you a way to back out of the deal without losing your earnest money. Second, add a line stating, "This offer is contingent upon the buyer's full approval of the financing terms." Third, if the property falls under a Homeowners Association add a line stating, "The seller shall supply the buyer with an updated copy of the By-Laws from the Homeowners Association and those By-Laws must be approved by the buyer." The reasoning behind this is to ensure the Home-owners Association allows rentals. You will also want to arrange for a closing date between the 15th and 20th of the month to give you more time before your first mortgage payment is due, usually about 45 days after the signing.

As part of a standard real estate purchase contract, earnest money – a deposit put down to hold the property – is usually a requirement from the seller. The amount is negotiable between the buyer and the seller. As a buyer (investor) you will want to limit your risk by putting down the least amount of earnest money as possible. You can lose your earnest money if you back out of the purchase.

Understanding Loans and Mortgages

Most people don't know that a mortgage is not a loan. Instead, a mortgage is a lien placed against your property. The bank or mortgage company does not own your property; they simply have a lien on your property that is called a mortgage. If you don't make your payments on the loan they have the legal right to enforce the lien on your property.

As an investor you will notice that the company who holds the original mortgage will usually be placed in the first position as the lien holder per the loan contract. This protects the mortgage holder if you default on the loan. To help you understand how this works read the following scenario:

Mr. and Mrs. Homeowner purchase a house for $100,000 and provide a 5 percent down payment ($5,000). Mortgage Company A lends the couple $95,000 (the other 95 percent). Two years later Mr. and Mrs. Homeowner decide to remodel the home and take out a second mortgage from Bank B. Mortgage Company A remains in the first position as a lien holder and Bank B will be in the second, or junior, position. If Mr. and Mrs. Home-owner default on the loan, Mortgage Company A will call the loan due and the house will be in foreclosure and sold. The proceeds from the sale will first go to pay off the lien holder in the first position (Mortgage Company A) and any money left over will go to the lien holder in the second, or junior, position (Bank B). Whoever is in the first position gets paid first. Most lenders will usually want to be in the first position as the lien holder.

Pay the Minimum

When searching for a loan, find a lender who will require the lowest down payment. You want to keep as much money in your pocket as you can.

For instance, let's assume you have $100,000 in cash to invest into real estate. You find an investment property for $100,000. You would have two questions on your mind: Should I pay cash?, or should I borrow the money and keep most of the cash in my pocket? Since the more cash you have, the more leverage you will have, the goal in real estate investing is to own as many investment properties as you can with positive cash flow. In order to accomplish this goal you would best be served by splitting the $100,000 into several down payments and buying several different investment properties.

An example scenario would be one in which you purchase nine investment properties at $100,000 each, putting a 10 percent down payment on each one. You will then have nine investment properties with a monthly cash flow, nine properties, appreciating and nine investment properties for tax benefits. You will also still have $10,000 left to put into your operating fund (cash reserves) for repairs and maintenance of the properties.

When you buy one investment property in full for cash you do have more monthly cash flow; however, your appreciation and tax benefits are for one investment property, not nine. In the long run, you will accumulate far more wealth with more properties. When you purchase an investment property with 10 percent down and the lender loans you the other 90 percent, you're the one who collects 100 percent of the appreciated value of the property and, if you decide to sell the property years later you will cash in on 100% of the property's appreciated value (equity).

"Your down payments are not tax deductible."

For example, let's say you buy an investment property for $100,000 with 10 percent of your own money ($10,000) as a down payment. The other 90 percent ($90,000) is borrowed from a lending institution in the form of a mortgage. After one year the investment property has appreciated 10 percent, and is now worth $110,000 and, in this scenario, you would have $20,000 in equity (not including any of the principal paid over the first year of the loan). In one year, your $10,000 investment has grown to $20,000 simply because of appreciation, giving you $20,000 to put in your pocket (minus the closing cost) if you decide to sell the property. You have doubled your money in one year. Now, imagine what would happen if you kept the property for three to five years (or if you have nine investment properties instead of one). Even though you put down only 10 percent of the purchase price for each property, as the investor you receive 100 percent of the appreciated value.

This becomes a prime example of using other people's money to better your financial future.

Monthly Cash Flow

When you get a loan you must decide how long you want to make payments before it is paid off. Generally speaking, you will have to choose between a 15-year or 30-year mortgage. I recommend the 30-year mortgage for a number of reasons. With a 30-year loan your payments are lower, thereby increasing your cash flow. This is important when your goal is to decrease your monthly debt and increase your cash flow. This also increases your ability to obtain future loans on investment properties. With a 15-year loan you will have higher monthly payments, higher monthly debt, less interest to write off on your tax returns, and less cash flow.

You will also come across programs to make bi-weekly mortgage payments. The claim behind bi-weekly mortgage payments is that you will pay off your mortgage faster and save on interest. By paying bi-weekly instead of monthly you make one extra monthly payment a year, which takes away from your cash flow one month out of the year. Also, since there are often extra fees involved with changing from monthly to bi-weekly mortgage payments, I would still opt for the 30-year loan with a monthly mortgage payment. After all, your tenants are paying for your mortgage while you're getting the tax benefits and positive cash flow, which is what will make you wealthy in the future.

Common Loan Types

The definitions of the loans discussed below are very basic and simplified to give you a limited understanding of their structure. When applying for a loan make sure you read and understand what is involved.

Conventional and Non-conventional Loans

Conventional loans – also known as conforming loans – are the most common loans used by small investors to buy residential property. Conventional loans have strict guidelines such as good credit scores, sufficient cash reserves, and low personal debt. The lenders use the same format and guidelines to qualify all borrowers for loan approvals so they can easily sell the loans on the secondary market. (The loans are usually sold as a bulk package, not individually.) This in turn frees up more of the lender's funds to make new loans. There are two major reasons lenders sell loans and turn around to make new loans again. First, when interest rates rise the lenders want to unload the loans with the lowest interest rates to open up funds to make new loans at higher interest rates. Second, the majority of mortgage interest is paid at the beginning of the loan. For instance, when you take out a mortgage the initial payments are mostly going toward the interest on the loan. As you make more payments the amount applied to interest decreases and the principal portion increases. Since lenders know most of their profit is made in the first seven to ten years of the loan, lenders make more money when they make new loans no matter what the interest rate is. This is also a reason why lenders are so eager to give you a loan or have you refinance your current loan.

"Conventional loans usually offer the lowest interest rates."

Another loan – known as a nonconforming (subprime) loan – is for people who have less than average credit scores or don't meet income guidelines for other loans. Lenders who offer nonconforming loans have their own individual guidelines.

Federal Housing Administration (FHA) Loans

FHA stands for the Federal Housing Administration. The FHA is a division of the U.S. Department of Housing and Urban Development (HUD). In order to cover their risk, the FHA does not lend the money but instead they insure the lender who makes the loan. FHA insured loans are for owner-occupied or primary residences and are not investor loans. HUD does have investor loan programs such as the 203(K) or the title 1 loan. The 203 (K) loan is aimed at investors who want to purchase and occupy a property while rehabbing it. A title 1 loan is for low-cost rehabbing only. You must keep in mind that HUD insures the lenders against loss but does not itself lend money.

Veterans Administration (VA) Loans

VA stands for Veterans Administration. As with HUD and FHA loans, the VA is a governmental agency that insures the loan but it does not lend money. This program is for military veterans who qualify.

Commercial Loans

Commercial loans are usually for larger properties such as multi-family properties (with five or more units), office buildings, and stores. Depending on lenders' guidelines (which vary), these loans usually start out at $300,000. Most commercial lenders are more concerned with the financial viability of the property than the buyer. Commercial lenders will expect you to have large cash reserves on hand and a down payment of 20 to 50 percent of the purchase price. Make sure you have an attorney who is familiar with commercial loans before getting into commercial loans or property. It would be in your best interest to gain experience with the residential market first.

Adjustable Rate Mortgages (ARM)

ARMs are a type of loan that has a lower initial interest rate that becomes flexible after a certain period of time. The most common ARMs used are the 7-year ARM (7/1 ARM), 5-year ARM (5/1 ARM), 3-year ARM (3/1 ARM), and 1-year arm (1/1 ARM). Because most investors are likely to refinance properties every three to seven years, as an investor you should consider ARMs. The purpose of refinancing is to cash out your earned equity and purchase more real estate investments with your increased cash reserves. (Refinancing techniques will be explained later in this chapter.) Used correctly, ARMs can give you a lower monthly payment. If you anticipate refinancing before your interest rate becomes flexible the ARM may be a good financial tool for you to utilize.

"Look for built in prepayment penalties for ARM loans."

Balloon Loans

Balloon loans are usually used for short term lending (three to seven years). Investors may use balloon loans to lower their monthly payment. A majority or all of the payment in a balloon loan is for interest only, which means payments are insufficient to pay off the loan in full. The principal amount is due in one lump sum at the end of the loan. If you decide to get a balloon loan make sure you understand the terms and conditions involved. Since a balloon loan may be too complicated for beginners to grasp, you may want to consider an ARM loan. Their benefits are similar without taking on as much risk.

Loan Fees

Loan fees vary depending on your lender. Since it's an easy way for them to make more profit, some lenders add on unnecessary fees to force you to pay more for the loan. For you, this is a waste of your money. No matter what the lender calls the fees it charges you, calculate the total cost of the loan. It is in your best interest to compare lenders so you're not overcharged with phantom fees. Some of the fees that normally show up on your settlement statement include:

- Title insurance
- Document recording (deed)
- Closing fee
- Appraisal
- Credit report (inexpensive)
- Survey (seller pays)
- Prepaid interest
- Escrow reserves

Some of the most common phantom fees include:

- Application fee
- Underwriting fee
- Discount points
- Coping fees
- Wire/delivery fees

Discount points, or points, are paid to get a lower interest rate and for the most part they are a waste of money since all you are doing is paying interest up front. Each point is equal to 1 percent of the loan amount. When a lender advertises a $100,000 loan at 6 percent interest rate with two points it means you will pay an extra $2,000 at closing in order to obtain the loan at the advertised rate. Without paying any points on the same loan amount your interest rate will, at most, be 6½ to 7 percent. You should pass on paying points unless you anticipate keeping the loan for a very long time.

Yield Spread Premiums (YSP)

Mortgage brokers are provided with wholesale interest rates from lenders; however, brokers can charge customers a higher interest rate to offer lenders a larger profit. The lender in turn pays brokers a commission called a Yield Spread Premium. This premium will be listed as POC (paid outside of close) on your settlement statement document at the closing. Remember, brokers and bankers make their profit by charging you different types of fees. This is just another technique to make more profit at their end. For example, a lender may advertise an interest rate of 6 percent to the broker. The broker in turn charges the customers 6¼ percent on the same loan. The broker will then collect a Yield Spread Premium (commission) for the extra ¼ percent earned on behalf of the lender. This is why it helps to shop around and compare mortgage brokers.

Good Faith Estimate

Under federal law (RESPA), a good faith estimate must be provided to you from your lender when you apply for a loan. Make sure you review it carefully. Don't hesitate to question any charges you don't understand. Beware of lenders who add extra fees the day before or day of the closing. Always question lender or brokers on last-minute fees and get an explanation why there is a need for the additional fees.

Remember that you can cancel the closing if additional fees seem to be extreme or if you're not comfortable with the numbers. It is best to consult with an attorney in this situation.

Owner/Seller Financing

Owner or seller financing is when the owner carries all or part of the purchase price in return for payments from the buyer. This type of financing works well for investors who are having problems getting a loan, and when a seller finances the full amount of the purchase there are no loan costs which results in a quick closing. Although owner or seller financing is appealing for buyers, even the most motivated sellers may not be open to the idea.

Lines of Credit (LOC)

Lines of credit, such as a home equity line of credit, are common. Most people get a home equity loan or line of credit to pay off other debt or to buy big-ticket items, but this only keeps them in debt longer or, even worse, puts them deeper in debt. When used properly a line of credit can be an excellent financial tool for real estate investors. You should only use a line of credit for emergencies or quick cash (such as short-term financing) so you don't miss out on a good deal. The LOC should not be used as a long-term down payment for a number of reasons. First, you risk tying up your source of quick cash when you might need it for the next good deal. Second, it shows up on your credit report and increases your debt ratio. Third, the lender who gives you the line of credit will have a lien on your property. In the event that you default on the line of credit the lender can foreclose on your property. Normally the lender who provides you with your home equity LOC or equity loan will show up in the second, or junior, position as a lien holder. Since they can rapidly become a money pit, be careful when using a line of credit or credit cards. Remember that you are getting into the real estate investment business to build assets that give you cash flow, not gain more liabilities that take cash out of your pocket.

Insurance

I have already covered insurance in Chapter 5, "Building Your Team." Remember to look over your policy to make sure you have the proper coverage, the property address is correct, and that coverage starts the day you close. Avoid any gaps in your coverage between renewal periods.

Attorney

Have your attorney look over the purchase contract. He or she will advise you on what changes need to be made, if any.

Home Inspector

Arrange for a home inspection, especially if the property is old or appears to be in need of repair. My advice for beginners is to have an inspection each time you purchase a property. Eventually you will know what to look for, but until then use the service of a certified inspector. When purchasing an investment property you will be presented with opportunities and problems. In order to benefit from the opportunities, you must be able to solve the problems. Since violating laws or regulations can be costly if fines are imposed, don't violate any laws. Furthermore, criminal offenses can take your freedom away and be devastating to your family. This is why it is important to have investment properties inspected by certified home inspectors.

Closing the Deal

You are now at the point where you are ready to set the closing date. I've found that the best time to close is between the 15th to the 20th of the month since it gives you approximately 45 days to get the rental unit ready before your first mortgage payment is due. Don't let the title company tell you when you must close; the closing date must be mutually acceptable to both the buyer and the seller. In reality, the buyer has the most control due to the fact that nobody gets paid unless you or your attorney is at the closing.

Since I am on the subject of attorneys, I want to note that I always recommend new real estate investors use experienced real estate attorneys. Don't ever close without your attorney present, since he or she is essential to your success. You should use an attorney for any contracts you sign before or after the closing, thus ensuring the transaction will go smoothly.

At the closing you will be required to bring a certified bank check for any funds due. A personal check or cash will not be accepted at the closing. The title company will usually call you a day or two before the closing date to let you know how much you will owe at the closing. Since you will need time to get a certified check, if you don't hear from the title company by the day before the close, notify your attorney or the title company. In the event that you don't close on the property and need to redeposit the check, have it made out in your name and not the title company's name. At a successful closing the title company will have you endorse the back of the bank check in order for them to deposit it. Do not sign the check until you are at the closing and certain the closing is going through.

The title company requires all buyers and sellers to bring picture identification. Normally a driver's license or a state identification card will suffice. You may want to bring a receipt showing that insurance on the property has been paid for one year. Once you are at the closing the title company will request your identification, bank check, and a copy of your insurance (if needed). Your real estate attorney will walk you through all of the paperwork. During the closing is when you should ask questions about any paperwork you don't understand. (After all, you are the one who is signing it.) Be sure all of the information on the paperwork is correct, such as the spelling of your name, the property's address, and your social security number. Keep in mind that you want your mailing address to be your P.O. Box, not the address of the property you're purchasing. Any errors found should be corrected by crossing out the incorrect information and writing the correct information next to it. You will also want to get into the habit of initialing any changes made on paperwork you have signed, including the real estate purchase contract.

When you are finished with the paperwork you will be given copies of everything you have signed. It is important that you also get a copy of the survey and the appraisal for your records. Your attorney may want to keep one or both of them filed at his office; however, if you are organized it is better to have them in case you need them. Since you are the one who has paid for the services, it is your decision where to keep the survey and the appraisal.

Refinancing Your Property

In the future you may want to take advantage of refinancing to expand your investments. Depending on the market trends in your area, it can take between three and seven years to build a sizable amount of equity through appreciation. You may want to refinance to use the equity in your current property as a down payment for a new property or obtain extra cash to put into your operating fund (reserve fund). Because it is a loan, the money will be tax free; however, when you go to sell that property, the cash out refinancing may come into play at tax time. Check with your accountant or tax advisor to make sure you understand all of the implications of refinancing.

Let's say that you own a property appraised at $100,000 and you still owe $70,000. This means you can refinance and take up to $30,000 cash out at closing. (Don't forget to factor in the closing costs.) These figures are for obtaining a 100 percent loan-to-value mortgage on your property, which you may not want to do. Since your mortgage on the refinanced property will increase, causing your monthly payment to rise, be careful not to wipe out all of your monthly cash flow on that property. With this in mind, in this hypothetical situation I would refinance and cash out $20,000, leaving 10 percent equity in the property. I would have a $20,000 check, minus closing costs, to purchase a new investment property. If I planned correctly I might even have a few thousand dollars to add to my operating fund (also known as cash reserves). If you are going to refinance and cash out at closing make sure you come up with a detailed plan on the transaction's cost effectiveness to make sure it will be financially beneficial and worthwhile.

The 1031 Exchange

I will briefly discuss the Internal Revenue Code, Section 1031. This gives you another option if and when you decide to sell or upgrade your investment property. Since a 1031 exchange lets you sell your current investment property and roll your profit into another investment property, you can defer paying taxes on the profit from sale. However, you must use all of the profit from the sold property and roll it into the new property within 180 days of the closing or pay a capital gains tax on what you keep. If you need cash and want to defer paying taxes, refinance the new property after you purchase it.

If you are going to do a 1031 exchange it is best to let the title company and Realtor know ahead of time. This way they can file the proper paperwork and make preparations to get an exchange agent to hold the profit until you find a replacement property to roll the money into. It is also in your best interest to consult with your accountant or legal advisor before pursuing a 1031 exchange.

7

Preparing for Tenants

Now that you own a property it is time to get it ready to produce cash flow. In this chapter, I will address the steps necessary to find prospective tenants so you can choose from the most suitable applicants. Taking these steps will also help increase the value of your property.

Appearance

Your property must be thoroughly cleaned both inside and out. You can choose to do the cleaning yourself or hire a cleaning service. If you decide to hire a cleaning service, advise them that you are a real estate investor looking for a cleaning service to handle your properties when necessary. This will usually prompt the cleaning service to give you a discount and offer you their best service. They know that if you are impressed with their service you will give them future business and referrals. Keep in mind that when prospective tenants come to look at the rental unit they will get an idea of what you expect from them by how clean and well maintained the property is.

Painting

You should have all of the rooms in the rental property repaired and painted. In order to decrease future costs, the rooms should all be painted the same color. Pick a color that is easy to match, such as white. This will save you time if you have to do any touch ups in the future. You want your property to look clean and well maintained. Although painting is something you can do yourself, it is harder work than most people realize and very time consuming and so you may want to consider hiring someone else to do the job. Based on my experience, I would suggest hiring painters if you can afford to do so. It will save your back, your time, and your mind. When hiring any kind of service, don't forget to mention that you are a real estate investor. They will do their best to please you in hopes of getting your future business.

Amenities

In order to protect your investment, there are certain amenities you want to put into your rental property. While tenants will be under the impression that you put these amenities in for their comfort and convenience, amenities are beneficial for you as well. Many investors will not spend money to add amenities to their properties because they want to cut down on costs or avoid complaints about needed repairs. If you correctly maintain the property, you will not have to concern yourself with those problems. The most costly amenities you will purchase are appliances such as refrigerators, stoves, and washing machines and dryers. I recommend that you supply at least these appliances for your tenants. You will eventually notice that the most costly damage is caused when tenants move in or out or when a faulty appliance leaks water that goes undetected for a long period of time. If you do not provide appliances, you may have tenants leave their old appliances behind. To avoid these types of headaches, and because most tenants are willing to pay more for extra conveniences, it is in your best interest to supply well-maintained appliances to the tenant. For obvious reasons, you should also supply a fire extinguisher in the kitchen area. Providing wall hangers for putting up pictures will keep damage to walls to a minimum. Buying a case of furnace filters for the tenants every year ensures that the furnace filter is being replaced correctly. These items should all be written into the lease and the move-in inspection report.

You must dare to be different and stand away from the crowd. Build your reputation as a professional investor, not some fly-by-night landlord. Keep your properties up to date, clean, painted, and well landscaped. Before you know it you will have a waiting list of suitable tenants and your current tenants will take good care of your property with the intention of staying a long time.

Photos and Video

Once you have your rental property ready for tenants you will want to take photos or videotape the premises. Take the photos or video before the lease signing and make sure all repairs and cosmetic touchups are performed before taking photos or video footage so that any damage to the premises can be documented. I also have a check box on the move-in inspection report (see "Appendix A" for a sample form) that specifies whether photos or videos were taken of the premises. New tenants will sign a move-in inspection report and receive a copy for their own records. Store your move-in inspection photos or videotapes in a safe place for future reference.

Setting the Rent

Setting the amount of rent to charge can be tricky. Investors generally use the one percent rule as a guideline, which means you set the rent by determining one percent of the total value of the property. For example, if you have a townhouse with a value of $150,000, one percent (or the monthly rent) would be $1,500. Remember that this method is only a guideline and you will need to find out what the going rent is in the area on the same type of property. You can find this information in local newspapers, from a Realtor or management company, or by researching rentals on the Internet. Be aware of the fact that appliances, utilities, and certain upgrades will bring in higher rents. By research-ing trends in the area you should be able to choose a fair market rent. Investors will usually test the rental market by setting the rent toward the higher end of the scale. If the property remains vacant, the asking rent will be decreased until a suitable tenant is found.

Security Deposits

You will want to set your tenants' security deposit at a minimum of one month's rent. You may want to collect a larger than usual security deposit from prospective tenants who have a less-than-average credit rating. Once you choose the most suitable tenant have them write a check from their checking account for the security deposit. Make a copy of the check, front and back, before you deposit it. The reason for this is so you have the tenant's bank account inform-ation on file. In the future you may have to take legal action against the tenant, so it's best to be prepared. Make sure the check clears before you have the tenant sign the lease. This will be explained in more detail later in this chapter.

Finding the Right Tenants

Having the right tenants makes the difference between loving real estate and hating it. A majority of potential problem tenants should be eliminated in the screening process. This section of the book will teach you how to locate good tenants and screen out problem tenants. You will be amazed at how well the following techniques work when applied correctly. Besides it's better to have no tenant than to have a problem tenant.

Newspaper Ads

Believe it or not, the screening process starts with the newspaper ad. Simply by the way your ad is worded, you can eliminate 80 to 90 percent of problem tenants. Furthermore, you don't want your time wasted on people looking for a hand out or trying to take advantage of you. Keep in mind that it's not the quantity of potential tenants that apply, but the quality of tenants that counts.

Your ad should state the basic details about your property such as the number of bedrooms, bathrooms, location, rent, and type of housing, appliances, and a contact number. To assist you with the screening process you will want to add that a credit check will be done. Keep the ad short and to the point.

>
> *Example:* Chicago, 3 Bd, 1.5 Ba,
> TH, 2c gar, W&D, Credit ck, $1500,
> 555-555-5555
>
> *Long form:* Chicago, 3 Bedrooms,
> 1½ bathrooms, Townhouse, 2 car
> garage, washer and dryer, credit
> check, $1,500.00 monthly.

Most people with bad credit won't even call when they see that a credit check is required. The ones that do call will usually be honest about their bad credit and tell you, which will give you the opportunity to screen them over the phone and therefore save your valuable time.

Answering the Calls

My experience has proven that only one out of five people who make an appointment to see a rental property will show up. In order to keep prospective tenants from wasting your valuable time running back and forth to the rental property, your time will be better served if you set a day and a window of time in which you will be showing the property. Avoid making special arrangements to meet prospective tenants at their convenience. More times than not they either won't show up or they will not financially qualify to rent the property.

You will want to advise any prospective tenants that there is an application fee and that a credit check will be done. Set your application fee to at least cover your cost for the credit check and the necessary forms. Remind them that the application fee is non-refundable and you will only take cash. Be straightforward with all the callers and don't deviate from your procedures. You are looking to find the best qualified and most suitable tenant. This may take time, but it will be worth it in the long run.

Showing the Rental Property

As previously stated, on average only one in five people will show up to view the property. Because it only takes one good tenant to rent your property, don't become discouraged. The following is a basic checklist of what you need to make your first showing a success.

- All repairs and painting should be completed
- Dress professionally
- Show up early
- Open the blinds and turn on all the lights
- Extra applications, pens, and clipboards
- Some cash at hand to make change and cash receipts

- Information sheets with schools, shopping, hospitals, etc.

In the future you may find more items to add to your checklist, but for now this will get you started. Since punctuality is a good characteristic to look for in a tenant, get to the property early to see which prospective tenants show up early. Once prospective tenants are in the door, greet them and answer their questions. Unless they request a tour of the property, let them walk through the property alone. When they are finished ask them if they would like to fill out an application. Explain to them that you will offer the property to the first qualified applicant. Remember to number the applications in the order of when prospective tenants arrived and make sure you collect the application fee. See "Appendix A" for a sample application.

Screening Prospective Tenants

The purpose of screening potential tenants is to avoid problems in the future. In order to avoid accusations of unfair treatment and dis-crimination, the screening process should be conducted in the same manner every time. It is extremely important to do credit checks on all potential tenants. Don't pass this step up because you feel it is not worth the time or the effort. Once you are affiliated with a credit agency, the process is simple and quick.

Most credit agencies will have you fill out an application and may ask you to pay a one-time application fee. They will usually fax a credit report to you within an hour or two after your request. In addition to telling you whether a potential tenant pays his or her bills on time, the credit report also gives you a standard that can be used to rank potential tenants.

Other subjects you may want to consider include whether potential tenants smoke, if they have pets (and what kind), and how many cars they own. These are just some of the questions you may want to add to your application form to assist you with the screening process.

Call prospective tenants' current landlord to see what information you can get on their past history. Since some landlords may lie to get rid of their problem tenants, be cautious with what the current landlord tells you. A good practice is to make a list of questions to ask the current landlord and write down his or her answers. Then ask your potential tenant the same questions and compare the answers. If your intuition is telling you that something isn't right you may want to move on to the next applicant.

Once you find tenants that you are satisfied with, contact them to see if they are still interested in the property. Tell them they are No. 1 on the list of qualified applicants and that the rental unit is open if they want it. You will need to meet with your new tenant to get the security deposit. Generally, the best place to meet with them is at their current residence or your rental property. The advantage of meeting a new tenant at their current residence is that you get to see how they keep their house.

The security deposit should be in the form of a check written from the tenant's personal checking account. Set up the lease signing for no less than one week after you receive the security deposit check so you have time to photocopy both sides of the check and make sure it clears. Advise the new tenants that their check has cleared and they should bring first month's rent (in the form of cash or a money order) to the lease signing.

Signing the Lease

At the lease signing have the tenants walk through the property to make sure it is in a mutually acceptable condition. Briefly go over the move-in inspection report with the tenants and have them sign it. In order to make sure the tenant understands all aspects of the lease, go over the lease line by line. Since you don't want to go through the time and trouble of reviewing the lease in detail before getting the first month's rent, collect it before signing the lease agreement with the tenant. This way, if the tenant doesn't have the rent or has a problem with the lease, you're better off moving on to the next potential tenant on the list.

"Consider giving the tenant a discount for rent payments that are received early."

It will also be to your advantage to bring at least three copies of every form to be signed: one for you, one for the tenant, and one for any mistakes you may make. A laptop and portable printer combination is a convenient alternative to print your forms; however, the cost in the start up phase of your real estate investment business is always an issue.

Tenant's Packet

A tenant's packet should contain the following items:

- Copy of the lease
- Copy of the move-in inspection report
- Pre-addressed envelopes for payment
- Monthly payment coupons (1 year)
- Homeowners Association rules & policies (by-laws)
- Neighborhood information sheet (schools/churches/hospitals)
- Work order request sheets (for repairs)
- Contact phone numbers
- Utility phone numbers such as gas, electric, cable, and phone
- Location sheet for water shut off/smoke detectors/fuse panel.

8

Managing Tenants

Because situations involving tenants can become stressful if not handled properly, in this chapter you will learn simple techniques on how to manage your tenants and the problems that may arise. While your real estate investment property is yours you must nonetheless treat it like a business and not take problems personally. When you let this happen, you make decisions based on emotions. We all know of some people and maybe ourselves who have made emotional decisions in which we regretted later. If you use knowledge rather than emotions to make decisions you will consistently come up with well developed and concise solutions to your problems. In some circumstances it may be necessary to call on the services of a professional from your real estate investment team to deal with certain problems. This may cost you more money now, but it will be worth it in the long run.

Anyone dealing with a business expects it to be handled in a professional manner. As an investor you must treat your tenants to the same professional courtesy you would expect to receive. It is possible to be kind and firm when dealing with your tenants. Have integrity, be honest, and most importantly keep your word.

The best way to avoid problems is to do what you can to prevent them. Below, I have listed some of the most common and overlooked areas for potential problems. This list does not cover everything, but it will help you troubleshoot your relationship with your tenants. You may even want to add some of the following criteria to your rental lease.

Tenant Grading

Develop a grading system for your tenants. I use A thru E, with A being the best grade and E (eviction) being the worst. Take into account late payments, damage done to the property, cleanliness, and complaints. This will give you a system by which to evaluate your tenants and will assist you in deciding whether to renew a lease, how much to increase the rent, where to place new appliances, and what upgrades to perform. At lease signings I advise my new tenants of the grading system and explain to them how it is implemented. Tenants learn very quickly that grade A and B tenants earn special privileges.

Collecting Rent

You have two options in the way you collect rent. The first option is to have the tenants mail their rent checks to your P. O. Box. The second option is for you to pick up the rent every month. There are advantages and disadvantages to both.

Having the tenants mail their rent checks to your P.O. Box will make it easy for you to pick up the checks at a central location, thus cutting down on time, gas, and mileage costs. You will also be able to pick up the checks at your convenience. The down side is that you won't see your rental property as often as you should and you will have limited contact with your tenants. I know some people find the idea of limited contact with your tenants appealing; however, contact keeps you informed about what is happening with your tenant and the rental property. The expectation of your visit every month will force tenants to keep the rental property in order.

In addition to giving you contact with your tenants, picking up the rent in person allows tenants to pay cash. Paying cash is a benefit if you have a tenant who bounces checks or is constantly late with their rent. Another advantage to collecting the rent in person is that tenants have the opportunity to voice their concerns on such issues as repairs, hazards, or other problems. You don't want to be in a situation where a tenant files a complaint against you for a local code violation. This is more likely to happen if a tenant claims they rarely have contact with you. If you decide to have limited contact with the tenants make sure you provide a sufficient supply of work order repair forms (see "Appendix A" for a sample form) to your tenants. Ideally, you will supply them with enough to last the length of their lease.

Late Fees

Follow the lease your tenants signed. If it states late fees will be assessed, assess them. If you waive late fees once, most courts will consider them waived for the life of the lease. Even worse, tenants will be under the impression that the lease no longer applies to them. If you ever decide to change any part of the lease you and your tenants signed, you should write an addendum to protect your legal rights to enforce the lease.

As a side note: The lease must be signed by both you and the tenant to be valid and binding. My advice is to act on any lease violations by sending a letter of violation (see Appendix A) to the tenant.

Repairs and Maintenance

Repairs can quickly drain your operating fund. The best way to keep repair costs down is to keep a maintenance schedule on all appliances, the furnace, any air conditioning units, and anything else regularly used by the tenant. You will notice that some tenants take care of amenities while others do not. To combat this problem it is good to have a clause in the lease that states all minor repairs are the responsibility of the tenants. As an alternative to making your tenants responsible for all costs, you can also write the clause in a manner that stipulates the tenant is responsible for the first $75 of a repair. This should not include normal maintenance costs. A repair fee will keep tenants from abusing the property and its appliances. If they are grade A or B tenants, you can advise them that it is customary to waive the repair fee. This will act as an incentive for tenants to take care of the premises.

Inspections

Inspections are critical and should be done at least once a year. Most investors will perform inspections at the time the lease is renewed. The scope of the inspection should be thorough. You want to prevent unnecessary damage or repair calls by catching a problem early. Areas you particularly want to focus your attention on are:

- Water pipes, drains, and hoses
- Hot water heater
- Furnace
- Toilets
- Windows
- Doors
- Electric outlets and switches
- Smoke detectors

Make sure to spend a little extra time when examining areas that have the potential to cause water or fire damage since these can be very costly to repair.

Utilities

Tenants should pay for all of the utilities they use. Whenever possible, supply new tenants with contact numbers for utility services and don't forget to notify the utility companies to stop service if you have them under your name. For my multi-unit properties I have made it a habit to look for properties that have separate utility meters for each unit. Commonly, in multi-family properties you will find one boiler supplies heat to all of the units. You will have to average this cost into the rents so you don't lose money during the cold months. See to it that your lease includes a section on what utilities the tenant will be responsible for.

"Compare the utility meter numbers with the meter numbers on your account statement to make sure they match."

Homeowners Association (HOA)

Many homes are under HOAs. If this applies to your property, supply the tenant with a copy of the rules and regulations or By-laws of the HOA. You will want to add a stipulation to the lease regarding the tenants' adherence to the HOA By-laws.

Lockouts

Lockouts should be included in the lease just in case tenants lock themselves out of the property. Make it the tenant's responsibility to pay for a locksmith and any damage caused. You should charge a fee if you have to take the time to perform the open-up yourself.

Pets

Your lease should specify what types of pets are allowed, if any. Since most tenants have a pet of some sort, you may want to adopt some type of guideline on pets or you may risk eliminating a large pool of potential tenants. In addition, local governments are starting to recognize the rights of pet owners as tenants.

Waterbeds

Waterbeds are heavy and could cause major damage if they spring a leak. Make a provision in your lease that no waterbeds are allowed in the rental property.

Phone

Make sure you have an updated phone number for your tenants on file. It is the tenant's responsibility to notify you of any changes.

Insurance

Advise the tenant that they will need to have renters' insurance if they want to protect their personal property from damage or loss. Your insurance on the rental property will not cover the tenant's personal property.

Subletting

Also commonly known as subleasing, this should be prohibited and stated so in the lease. Subletting is when you rent the property to a tenant who turns around and rents the same property to a third party.

Attorney Fees

Place a sentence in your lease that stipulates the tenant is responsible for any legal fees incurred to enforce the lease.

"Always review the lease before you go to the lease signing."

The aforementioned items deal with protecting yourself from irresponsible tenants. However, you will want to take the time and money to make life better for your good tenants. One of the ways I do this is to send cards on tenants' birthdays. (You should have personal information, such as birth dates on their rental application.) I also send out Christmas cards with a partial rent refund check or a gift card. It is important to treat your tenants like business clients. This will give you a more professional relationship with the tenants. Do not ever become personal friends with your tenants. Business and pleasure should not be mixed or it can potentially result in financial disaster.

Hiring a Property Management Company

Management companies are great if you don't want to deal with your tenants. Their fees usually are equal to one month's rent per year. Before you sign a contract agreeing to their services, it is imperative that you understand what the management company is responsible for. As an investor you should shop around to learn what services most management companies customarily offer.

Government Assisted Housing

Most investors cringe when government assisted housing (commonly known as section 8) is mentioned. They will tell you all of the reasons you should not accept people on section 8. The only question you have to ask them is how many people on section 8 they have rented to. Chances are very high they will reply, "None, but I heard..." You can figure out the rest. Smart investors will thoroughly research a subject to see if it will be financially viable. Don't take other people's opinion as fact; find out for yourself. I will tell you that I have personally rented too many families on government-assisted housing programs. And have found that when they are properly screened – as all potential tenants should be – they present little or no problem. In reality, it has been my experience that if you give them a nice place to live in they usually take better care of it than tenants who pay their rent without government assistance.

> ### "Knowledge used correctly is a powerful asset."

To give you a basic understanding on how government assisted housing programs work I have broken the process into four sections: approved rental, payment structure, screening stage, and receiving payment.

Approved Rental

You must first notify the housing authority in your area that you have a property to rent and are willing to take government-assisted tenants. The housing authority will ask how many bedrooms are in the unit and how much are you asking for rent. While the rent should be set at the going rate for the area, be prepared to be flexible. The housing authority will set up a date and time to inspect the unit for habitability.

Payment Structure

A few days after your unit passes the inspection you will be notified with the amount of rent the housing authority is willing to pay. You don't have to settle for the amount offered. You can try to negotiate a higher amount. The housing authority uses a formula – known as Fair Market Rent (FMR) – set by HUD (the Department of Housing and Urban Development). HUD breaks the country down into regions and determines the average rent paid for that area (usually by the county) and the number of bedrooms in the unit. The problem with this formula is that it is always a least one year behind the going market rent when it is posted. You can find the FMR on the HUD Web site.

The benefit of the government-assisted housing program is that you can accept the rent payment offered or rent the unit out to a tenant not on government assistance. For instance, if the housing authority offers you $1,000 a month for rent and you find a regular tenant willing to pay the going rate of $1,150 you can still rent to that person. The acceptance of the rental amount offered by the housing authority does not obligate you to only rent to government-assisted tenants. However, once a lease is signed by a government-assisted tenant, you are required to carry out the lease until the expiration date.

Screening Stage

Government-assisted tenants are screened in the same manner as any other potential tenant. But keep in mind that the housing authority will be paying the bulk of the rent and the tenant will pay the remaining balance. You are not to charge the tenant any more rent than the housing authority has an agreement for. The assisted tenants will have vouchers stating how many bedrooms they are eligible for and the percentage of the rent for which that the housing authority is responsible. The housing authority's calculations are based on the tenant's income and the number of children in their custody or care.

Receiving Payment

Depending on where you live, the housing authority will either mail you a check or directly deposit the rent into your bank account. As long as there are no deficiencies in the rental unit, you are sure to get paid at the same time every month whether it is through a paper check or direct deposit. As far as the tenants' share of the rent, it is up to you to decide what forms of payment are acceptable.

The operation of government assisted programs may vary depending on the area in which you invest. It is best if you contact the nearest agency to find out their criteria. Having government-assisted tenants can work to your advantage. It is up to you to research the situation to see if there is an opportunity for you to increase your cash flow with less risk. Make your decisions based on investment knowledge and experience, not other people's opinion.

A Solution for Evictions

As an investor you may need to have a tenant removed due to lease violations, most often for nonpayment of rent. In this situation you have two ways to approach the problem. First, you can elect to start legal proceedings for an eviction. Alternatively, you can come up with a solution that will, in the end, benefit the both of you. After all, your goal is to get the delinquent tenant out so you can rent the property to a paying tenant. The problem with legal proceedings is that they cost money and take time, leading to hostility between you and the tenant. The time factor may also give disgruntled tenants an opportunity to damage the rental property. Taking legal action against a tenant should be used as a last resort.

In my experience, I have found that the best approach is to give the tenant a choice on how they want to move out of the rental property. The first choice is to offer the tenant cash to move out. While it may seem counterintuitive, you will be paying the tenants with money from their own security deposit. The second choice is to face legal action and debt collections. When you force tenants to choose between receiving cash to be out within 48 hours or face legal proceedings, they opt for the cash. Furthermore, most delinquent tenants have enough sense to realize when to call it quits and move out. Whatever you do, don't negotiate the amount due with the tenant or they will continue to put off the move to get more cash from you that they don't deserve anyway. The key to making this work to your advantage is to enforce lease violations in a timely manner. When possible try to find a mutually agreeable solution to the problem before taking legal action. It is usually more cost effective and much quicker than the court system.

9

Protecting Your Investment with an LLC

In a previous chapter I advised you to have different types of insurance policies to help protect your real estate investments and personal property. As you know, frivolous liability lawsuits are on the rise. Juries are awarding large sums of money to so-called victims who appeared to have had a lack of common sense during the incident leading to the lawsuit. Furthermore, there are many lawyers who are willing to go to great lengths to take away from honest and hardworking people who have built a better future for themselves. This is why you must protect your assets by educating yourself. Learn from other investors' mistakes so you won't have to learn from your own.

"Continue to build your knowledge."

In my opinion, a Limited Liability Company (LLC) is the best type of business under which to hold your real estate investments. I will discuss the basics of LLCs so you will have a limited understanding on what an LLC is and how it can protect your real estate investments. I do, however, suggest that you hire an attorney and research what is expected of an LLC in the state in which you wish to operate the company.

What is an LLC?

LLC stands for Limited Liability Company. While the LLC is a fairly new business concept in the United States, European countries have been using this business form for a long time with great success. This prompted individual state governments in the United States to find new ways to develop better business forms.

The Internal Revenue Service only recognizes two major types of business forms: partnerships and corporations. Both types have their own drawbacks such as double taxation (corporations) and no limited liability protection (partnerships). State governments decided to take the most attractive aspects of partnerships and corporations to develop what is now known as the Limited Liability Company. Most business owners praised the new form of business and many even believe LLCs are the future of business.

Holding your real estate investments under an LLC allows you to operate it like any other business. State LLC acts now give business owners limited liability, flexible management, pass-through taxation, and no restrictions on who the owners can be. No other business form can match the unique qualities of an LLC. The LLC can have an unlimited number of owners and can be member-managed (owner) or manager-managed. A member-managed LLC lets its members have a voice on how the LLC is operated, while a manager-managed LLC lets members choose the manager and the number of managers they want to run day-to-day operations. The managers chosen don't have to be members of the LLC. With an LLC you can give your managers or members titles such as President, Vice-President, Chief Executive Officer (CEO), or Chief Financial Officer (CFO). The titles can define who has ranking power and what their job entails.

Why Use an LLC?

The greatest features of an LLC are its limited liability protection, flexible management, and flow-through taxation. The limited liability factor will protect you from being personally liable for any lawsuits brought against your LLC. In other words, if a tenant sues the LLC they can't go after your house or other personal property unless they too are under the same LLC. You can even place every property you purchase under a separate LLC to give you protection for each individual property.

Flexible management refers to the ability to organize and operate the LLC as you see fit. As mentioned above, you can have the members manage the LLC or you can choose to hire managers to manage the LLC. The members can put a limit on how much authority managers have to make decisions or bind the LLC and can also control how much voting power each member will have based on their percentage of ownership or whatever formula is set forth in the Operating Agreement. (The Operating Agreement will be discussed later in this chapter.)

From a business standpoint, flow-through taxation is desirable. An LLC is usually taxed as a partnership under IRS guidelines. Partnerships have flow-through taxation, which means owners are taxed on their individual income tax returns. The LLC can make a disbursement of funds to its members and the LLC is not taxed. The members who receive the funds must then report it as income on their individual income tax returns.

If your LLC were to be taxed as a corporation by the IRS you would be taxed twice. When a corporation disburses funds, those funds are taxed. When the owners, often known as shareholders, receive those disbursed funds they must report them as capital gains on their individual income tax returns. This is what the business world refers to as double taxation. For tax purposes it is more advantageous for your

LLC to be taxed as a partnership and not as a corporation. The differences between a partnership and a corporation as defined by the IRS will be explained in more detail later. This will help you understand how the IRS determines if your LLC is taxed as a partnership or a corporation.

Another good feature of an LLC is gifting ownership interests for estate planning. Under the LLC a parent can gift ownership interests to a child and still retain control over the LLC. This is possible even if the child holds a larger percentage of the ownership interests than the parent. The parent can choose to have the Operating Agreement reflect that the parent is the manager of the LLC with 100 percent of the voting rights.

How to Form an LLC

Since starting up an LLC is a big step for most people, I highly recommend hiring an attorney or accountant to help you with the process, especially since state law requires your company to designate an agent for service of process (such as your attorney) who will be served any legal notices on behalf or against your company. The purpose of this is so you can't hide your company in the event that legal action is taken against your LLC and a summons must be served. The agent you name in your Articles of Organization will be the one who is served any legal notices or summons on your LLC's behalf. It is your responsibility to keep your contact information current with your agent, especially since when your agent is served with any legal notice or summons your LLC will be considered served even if your agent is unable to locate you.

To officially start up your LLC you or your attorney must file Articles of Organization and an Operating Agreement with the state in which the LLC will be based. The Articles of Organization are a one or two page document stating the LLC's name, address, date of organization, agent for service of process, how it will be managed, and that you are doing business in that state.

The Operating Agreement details how the LLC will be operated and managed and is a very important document which should detail every aspect of the company from member's responsibilities to fund disbursements. Again, this is an area where professional legal services are highly recommended. The Operating Agreement defines whether or not the LLC is taxed as a partnership or a corporation by the IRS.

Taxation of an LLC

For tax purposes, the IRS places all businesses with two or more owners under one of two business forms: partnerships and corporations. Depending on how your LLC is set up it will either be taxed as a partnership or a corporation.

The most desired business form to fall under is the partnership form since it offers the advantage of flow-through taxation. This means the LLC and the members are only taxed one time, as opposed to corporations in which the IRS practices double taxation.

The IRS has a standard formula that it follows in order to determine if your business is taxed as a partnership or corporation. The formula has four features:

1. Limited liability
2. Continuity of life
3. Centralized management
4. Free transferability of ownership

To fall under the partnership form of taxation your LLC must have no more than two of the four features. If the LLC has three or more of the features it will be placed under the corporation form of taxation by the IRS. The following is a basic explanation of the four features of the formula.

Limited Liability

Limited liability means that the members or managers cannot be held personally liable for the actions or involvement of the business. Under the corporation type of business there is limited liability. However, under the partnership type of business the owners or members can be held personally liable. The LLC was developed to give its members and managers limited liability even if it falls under the partnership type of taxation. Check with your legal advisor to determine what regulations your LLC must follow to keep its limited liability status.

Continuity of Life

The corporation type of business has continuity of life by the simple fact that it will not dissolve due to a change in ownership. The LLC, on the other hand, usually stipulates in its Operating Agreement that a change in ownership will cause the LLC to dissolve. However, the Operating Agreement can also state that the LLC shall not terminate if the other members agree to continue the business. This in effect causes the LLC to lack this corporation type of business feature.

Centralized Management

The corporation type of business is managed by a board of directors who make decisions for the corporation. This is considered to be centralized management by the IRS. The LLC has the flexibility to be managed by all of its members, designated members, or outside managers. If the LLC is member-managed it is considered to lack the centralized management feature. Manager-managed LLCs are considered to have centralized management unless the managers are all members and each owns at least 20 percent of the membership interest. Again, consult a legal advisor due to the constant changes in the law.

Free Transferability

The corporation type of business has free transferability in that a member or shareholder can freely sell, gift, or trade his shares to whomever he desires. The partnership type of business doesn't have this option. Under a partnership an owner must get approval from the other owners before he can give up his ownership interest. The other owners must also approve of the new owner before being brought into the partnership. Most LLCs are set up in a similar manner to partnerships when it comes to transferability of ownership interest. This will protect the LLC from being placed under the corporation form of taxation.

"The more knowledge you have, the more options you will be aware of."

The laws on partnerships and corporations are very complex. I have only given you a brief explanation of partnership and corporation features that determine the LLCs form of taxation. It would be in your best interest to obtain professional legal advice if you decide to hold real estate under an LLC.

Bank Accounts

The LLC should always have its own bank account. No other accounts or funds should be commingled with the LLC bank account. When opening a bank account under an LLC the bank will usually request the following information or documents:

- Who will have signature authorization
- Operating Agreement
- Articles of Organization
- Federal Employee Identification Number (FEIN)

One Member LLCs

Some state's LLC acts allow one member LLCs. However, this may place your LLC under the corporation form of taxation (double taxation). Consider the fact that partnerships usually consist of two or more owners. Look at the possibility that the IRS may tax a one member LLC as a corporation even if your state's LLC act considers it a partnership type of business. To avoid any problems with taxation issues you may want to have at least two members in your LLC.

Flexible and Bulletproof LLCs

Every state has its own LLC act that stipulates whether the members (owners) can or can't choose what partnership or corporation features they want their LLCs to have. Each state has defined its LLC act as a flexible or bulletproof LLC.

Flexible LLCs

A flexible LLC is when the state's LLC act gives the members the flexibility to choose what partnership or corporation features they want their LLC to have. This also gives the members the option to be taxed as a partnership or corporation depending on how many and what features they choose to retain. The flexible LLC is a plus because its members can adjust the Operating Agreement to fit the needs of the company.

Bulletproof LLCs

A bulletproof LLC is when the state's LLC act restricts what partnership or corporation features an LLC can have. This is so the LLC will only be taxed under the partnership form of taxation and retains its limited liability status. States that impose the bulletproof LLC want to ensure that no LLC accidentally falls under the corporation form of taxation.

Transferring Ownership to an LLC

There are plenty of lenders out there who are not comfortable with loaning money to LLCs due to the limited liability factor. To get around this problem, you can purchase real estate investment property under your name then (after a period of time) transfer ownership of the property to the LLC. Just be aware of the "due on sale" clause in your mortgage note. The transfer of ownership may trigger this clause and cause the lender to call your loan due in full. However, even if the lender does have knowledge of the transfer of ownership they usually don't enforce the "due on sale" clause unless there is a delinquency in payment or interest rates have dramatically increased. Keep in mind that lenders make money by securing loans and would not benefit from a borrower leaving to refinance with another lender. As long as you're making your scheduled loan payments there is no reason for the lender to review your loan file. Nonetheless, you should consult with your legal advisor before making any changes in ownership.

Limited Liability Partnership (LLP)

LLPs closely resemble LLCs in that they both have limited liability, management flexibility, and flow-through taxation. LLPs require that there are at least two partners. Also the limited liability factor in the LLPs does not protect all of the owners in the same way that the limited liability factor in an LLC does. Partners in an LLP have individual limited liability protection, which means each partner is protected from another partner's negligent or damaging actions. If a lawsuit is filed, it is filed against the individual partners who are directly responsible for the negligent act. The other partners and the LLP as a whole are protected. You will find that LLPs are more suitable for professionals who offer services in which lawsuits are more prevalent. Once again, seek professional legal advice before making a decision about which business type to hold your real estate under.

Notes

10

Your Mental Attitude

At the time when I started to write this book I knew what I wanted to tell people, I didn't know how to get started or how to put my thoughts into words. Perhaps it was the fear that my thoughts would not be properly conveyed in writing, or that I would be criticized. The fear I speak of is in most of us. We all try to hide it by making excuses even though we know the excuses hold us back. There has been a first time for everything we have done in our lives, such as going to school, driving a car, that first kiss, and our first job. Why didn't fear stop us then? It's because our society expects these things from everyone. When someone tries to do something different (in the honest sense) other people tend to criticize or say they will fail. But when that someone succeeds where everyone said they would fail they are then considered to be a genius. I've got good news for you. If you don't let fear stop you, there's a genius inside of you just waiting to come out.

Now that you have acquired the knowledge to travel the financial path to success, there is one more characteristic that is a necessity. A "positive mental attitude" will give you an edge on your financial success and help you in every other aspect of your life. There are certain factors that form our personalities which are either positive or negative, but both cannot be present at the same time. The positive factors are desire (get it done), passion (love doing it), and persistence (never quit). The negative factors are fear (I'm afraid), fear (I can't change), and fear (what if I fail).

Fear has plagued man since the beginning of time. It destroys the human spirit that drives us. Fear is the dividing line between success and failure. Everyone has the fear of risk, criticism, and failure. Fear must be dealt with or you will not succeed. Look at the people around you, such as your relatives, co-workers, and friends. What do they say when you tell them you have a great idea such as starting your own business, investing, or acting on an invention? Do they reply, "It won't work" or, "It's a waste of time" or, better yet, tell you a story about someone who did that and failed? These types of comments are negative and are the products of fear. Don't let other people's fears and negative comments stop you from fulfilling your dreams. Look past them and avoid negativity at every turn or you will end up being your own worst enemy. Don't let time continue to pass or your passion and desire will fade away.

Write down your goals to get started. Complete them one by one and keep moving forward. That little monster called fear will be right behind you nipping at your heels. Pay it no attention, because it deserves none. You must remember that fear doesn't hunt alone. Fear hunts in a pack with other monsters such as negativity, procrastination, and dishonesty. Once one of these monsters take over your thoughts you're certain to fail.

"Be patient; know all the facts before you act."

As I have mentioned, your mind can only be in one mode at a time, positive or negative. The negative thoughts easily seep into your mind while positive thoughts must be interjected by force. You must work hard to train your mind to absorb and retain positive thoughts. Since negative thoughts lay dormant in your mind, seemingly waiting to appear, it is upon you to maintain positive thoughts. You will have to force yourself to think positively and over time it will become easier. You must train yourself to leave the negative pack of monsters behind and don't look back. A positive mental attitude will help you reach your goals and open your mind to new ideas and possibilities.

Previously, I had mentioned there are positive factors; desire, passion, and persistence. I am now going to discuss the meaning of these positive factors and why they are so important to you.

Desire

Desire is the overwhelming will to obtain what you crave. This is a very powerful emotion that will force you to accomplish the task at hand. It is like having an obsession for what you have set your sights on. Desire will carry you past the non-believers and those who feed on negativity and failure of others.

Passion

Passion is a must. Passion is a love of what you do. Matched with desire these two are nearly invincible. If you don't enjoy what you have chosen to undertake, you will not have peace of mind. You will look at the matter as an unpleasant task and it will inevitably fail. The passion for what you choose to do must be sincere to succeed.

Persistence

Persistence is the will to continue. You must never surrender yourself to quitting or giving up. When your path is blocked make a new plan and find an alternate path. The most successful people say they were closest to failure right before they succeeded. You must always have the drive to finish what you have started.

One Last Word

Be patient, don't expect instant results. Real estate investing takes time to grow. When you start it's like planting a seed. In the beginning this seed will have to be nurtured. But once it matures it will need less attention. You will be able to enjoy the rewards of your hard work and effort you have put into making your seed grow. Real estate investing is like that little seed. Done correctly and with patience your investment will grow strong. The time you take now to build a solid foundation will reward you many times over in the future. It is now up to you to take that next step and get started. Remember, have faith in yourself. Good luck on your journey.

<u>Notes</u>

Appendix A

Forms

Application to rent
Denial letter
Condition inspection report
Move-in information sheet
Settlement charges guide
Work order form
Notice of past due rent
Violation letter

Forms courtesy of The Landlord Protection Agency.

APPLICATION TO RENT
TENANT'S PERSONAL AND CREDIT INFORMATION
MUST BE FILLED OUT *COMPLETELY* TO BE PROCESSED

PERSONAL DATA:

NAME_____ BIRTHDATE_____ SOCIAL SECURITY# _____

DRIVERS LIC.# _____

NAME OF CO-TENANT_____ BIRTHDATE_____ SOCIAL SECURITY# _____

DRIVERS LIC.# _____

MAIDEN NAME OR ALIAS/ IF DIVORCED, PREVIOUS NAME _____

PRESENT ADDRESS_____ZIP_____ PHONE# _____

HOW LONG AT PRESENT ADDRESS_____ REASON FOR MOVING_____CURRENT RENT: $_____

CURRENT LANDLORD NAME _____PHONE#_____

PREVIOUS ADDRESS_____ZIP_____ PREVIOUS RENT:$_____

PREVIOUS LANDLORD NAME_____ PREVIOUS LANDLORD PHONE#_____

NUMBER OF OCCUPANTS _____ RELATIONSHIPS TO SELF_____
NUMBER OF OCCUPANTS WHO SMOKE_____ AGES_____
LIST ANY PETS_____NUMBER OF VEHICLES_____
CAR MAKE_____ YEAR_____ MODEL_____ COLOR_____ LIC.PLATE#_____
CAR MAKE_____ YEAR_____ MODEL_____ COLOR_____ LIC.PLATE#_____

OCCUPATION:

	PRESENT OCCUPATION	PRIOR OCCUPATION	CO-TENANT'S OCCUPATION
EMPLOYER			
SELF-EMPLOYED, D.B.A.			
BUSINESS ADDRESS			
PHONE			
POSITION HELD			
HOW LONG			
NAME AND TITLE OF SUPERIOR			
TYPE OF BUSINESS			
MONTHLY GROSS INCOME			

REFERENCES
PLEASE LIST AND INDICATE ALL SAVINGS (S) AND CHECKING (CK) ACCOUNTS

BANK NAME & BRANCH	ACCOUNT#	BALANCE	DATE OPENED	BANK PHONE

CREDIT BALANCES & OUTSTANDING LOANS

CREDITOR	ACCOUNT #	BALANCE OWED	DATE OPENED

PLEASE ATTACH ADDITIONAL INFORMATION IF ANY TO SEPARATE PAGE

I UNDERSTAND AND AGREE THAT SECURITY, 1ST MONTH'S RENT AND BROKER'S FEES MUST BE POSTED PRIOR TO THE EXECUTION OF A LEASE AGREEMENT IN CERTIFIED FUNDS, MONEY ORDER OR CASH.

LANDLORD/AGENT AGREES THAT THE DEPOSIT IS REFUNDABLE IF THE ABOVE APPLICANT IS NOT APPROVED, PROVIDING THAT THIS APPLICATION HAS BEEN FILLED OUT COMPLETELY AND TRUTHFULLY.
HAVE YOU OWNED A HOME IN THE PAST? _____. IF YES, HOW LONG? _____. HOW MANY? _____.
HAVE YOU EVER FILED A PETITION FOR BANKRUPTCY?_____ IF YES, WHEN?_____.
HAVE YOU EVER BEEN EVICTED FROM ANY TENANCY? _____.
HAVE YOU EVER WILLFULLY AND INTENTIONALLY REFUSED TO PAY RENT WHEN DUE?_____.

I HEREBY AUTHORIZE LANDLORD/AGENT TO VERIFY THE VALIDITY OF ALL THE ABOVE INFORMATION, AND TO INQUIRE WITH MY EMPLOYERS, FINANCIAL INSTITUTIONS, AND ANY OF THE CREDIT REPORTING BUREAUS AVAILABLE TO HIM. I AGREE TO SUPPLY ANY ADDITIONAL INFORMATION NEEDED BY OWNER/AGENT TO PROCESS THIS APPLICATION AND I ACKNOWLEDGE THAT MY DEPOSIT WILL BE FORFEIT IF I DO NOT COMPLY WITH ANY SUCH REQUEST. I AGREE THAT MY SCREENING FEE OF $25.00 *per adult applicant* IS NON-REFUNDABLE.
I HEREBY ACKNOWLEDGE RECEIPT OF A COPY OF THIS APPLICATION AGREEMENT. I AGREE THAT LANDLORD MAY TERMINATE ANY AGREEMENT ENTERED INTO IN RELIANCE ON ANY MISSTATEMENT MADE ABOVE. I DECLARE, UNDER PENALTY OF PERJURY, ALL OF THE ABOVE INFORMATION TO BE TRUE AND CORRECT, TO THE BEST OF MY KNOWLEDGE.

• APPLICANT_____ DATE_____

• APPLICANT_____ DATE_____

ATTENTION RENTAL AGENTS: SECURE YOUR TRANSACTION! **Before submitting, be sure you have:**
1. *Full required deposit by personal check made out to the owner.* 2. *Required screening fee.* 3. *Application completed in full.*

DEAR APPLICANT,

WE REGRET TO INFORM YOU, THAT YOUR RENTAL APPLICATION WAS
DECLINED FOR THE FOLLOWING REASON(S):

[   ] Applicant's price offer not accepted.

[   ] Rent/Income ratio does not meet minimum standards.

[   ] Lack of credit history, or derogatory information contained in credit report. See enclosed
       Adverse Action letter

[   ] Unable to obtain favorable current or past landlord reference.

[   ] Unable to verify current or past employment.

[   ] Applicant unable to comply with security deposit requirement.

[   ] Application was not accompanied by required screening fee.

[   ] Application contained false information. (False information on an application constitutes
       intent to defraud and perjury. Any deposits may be forfeit. Legal remedies may be
       pursued.)

[   ] Residence allows NO PETS.

[   ] Residence requires NO SMOKING.

[   ] Application submitted incomplete.

[   ] Intended occupancy date or lease term unacceptable.

We would like to thank you for the opportunity to review your rental application and hope
that we may be of service some time in the future.

RESPECTFULLY

Manager

Dear Applicant: Date:_____

Thank you for the opportunity to consider your application to rent. We regret we are unable to approve your application due to one or more of the following reasons.

According to the Fair Credit Reporting Act, you are entitled to know when adverse action was taken in whole or in part based on information received from a consumer reporting agency. Credit information having an adverse impact on your application was received from:

❑ One or more of the following consumer credit reporting agencies:

❑ Equifax Information Services
PO Box 105873
Atlanta, GA 30348-5873
(800) 685-1111

❑ Experian (TRW)
PO Box 2104
Allen, TX 75013-2014
(888) 397-3742

❑ Trans Union
PO Box 1000
Chester, PA 19022
(800) 888-4213
www.transunion.com\direct

The consumer credit reporting agencies only role was to provide credit information and cannot give the reason why your application was not approved.

Under the Fair Credit Reporting Act you have a right to receive a free copy of your credit report if one is requested within 60 days of this notice. You have a right to dispute the accuracy or completeness of any information in your credit file.

References and or information having an adverse impact on your application was received from:

❑ The following consumer reporting agency:
Agency:_____   Ph.#: _____

The Information Source's only role was to provide consumer report information and cannot give the reason why your application was not approved.

Under the Fair Credit Reporting Act you have a right to dispute the accuracy or completeness of any information in your consumer file. To do so you must contact the above consumer-reporting agency within sixty (60) days of receiving this notice.

❑ This adverse action was taken due to incomplete, inaccurate, or false information contained within the rental application.

CONDITION INSPECTION REPORT

TENANT(S)	PREMISES	
MOVE- IN DATE	MOVE-IN PHOTOS Y OR N	MOVE-IN VIDEO Y OR N
MOVE-OUT DATE	MOVE-OUT PHOTOS Y OR N	MOVE-OUT VIDEO Y OR N

The premises are being delivered in clean, sanitary, and good operating condition, with no spots, stains or damages, unless otherwise noted below in the "Move In Condition" box. If indicated above, the condition of the premises has been fully documented, dated, witnessed and verified on video tape and photographs.

AREA OR ITEM	CONDITION AT MOVE- IN	CONDITION AFTER MOVE- OUT	CHARGES
	√ = O.K.	√ = O.K.	

LIVING ROOM, DINING & HALLS
- Walls/Ceiling.......................................
- Floor/Carpet.......................................
- Closets/Doors/Locks..........................
- Lights/Mirrors....................................
- Window Treatments............................
- Windows/Screens...............................
- Fireplace(s)..

KITCHEN
- Walls/Ceiling/Floor.............................
- Countertops/Tile.................................
- Cabinets/Closets.................................
- Oven/Stove...
- Hood/Fan/Lights..................................
- Refrigerator..
- Dishwasher...
- Sink/Faucet/Disposal.........................
- Windows/doors/screens....................

BEDROOMS   (Specify BR # 1- 4)
- Walls/Ceiling.......................................
- Floor/Carpet.......................................
- Lights/Mirrors....................................
- Window Treatments............................
- Windows/Screens...............................
- Closets/Doors/Shelves.....................

BATHROOMS   (Specify # 1-4)
- Walls/Ceiling.......................................
- Floor..
- Cabinets/ Mirrors...............................
- Sink(s)...
- Tub/Shower...
- Tiles/Grout..
- Lights/Vent/Fan..................................
- Toilets..
- Windows/Doors ....
- Towel Bars/Accessories.................

- WASHER/DRYER...................................
- HEATING/AIR CONDITIONING.........
- BALCONY/DECK/PATIO.....................
- GARAGE(S)/STORAGE.......................
- GARAGE DOOR(S)...........................
- PARKING AREA...................................
- GARDEN/PLANTS/GRASS...............
- SMOKE DETECTOR............................
- NUMBER OF KEYS (SETS).............
- FENCES/GATES..................................

MOVE –IN COMMENTS

Tenant has inspected the above premises prior to occupancy and accepts it with the conditions and/or exceptions noted above. Tenant acknowledges this report as part of the lease with the Owner for the above premises. Tenant agrees to return the premises in like condition upon termination of tenancy, normal wear and tear excepted.

Tenant _____ Date _____ Tenant _____ Date _____

MOVE –OUT COMMENTS

CLEANING & OTHER CHGS	SECURITY SETTLEMENT	FORWARDING ADDRESS & PHONE #
GENERAL $_____ WINDOWS $_____ CARPET $_____ APPLIANCES $_____ GROUNDS $_____ GUTTERS $_____ DEBRIS $_____ PAINTING $_____ REPAIRS $_____ LATE FEES $_____ UNPAID RENT $_____ TOTAL $_____	TOTAL SECURITY DEPOSIT .... $_____ TOTAL CREDITS .... $_____ TOTAL CHARGES .... - $_____ BALANCE DUE FROM TENANT.. $_____ OR BALANCE DUE TO TENANT... $_____	_____ _____ _____ _____ *NEW PHONE #* REPORT PREPARED BY: _____ DATE:_____

Important Information for New Residence

Welcome! We wish you health and happiness in your new home. Listed below please find helpful information relating to your new residence.

Management : _____	Oil Co: _____
Police : _____	Water Co. : _____
Ambulance : _____	Telephone : _____
Fire Dept. : _____	Cable TV : _____
Electric Co: _____	Landscaper : _____
Gas Co : _____	Sanitation Dept. _____

Other Helpful Numbers

Plumber : _____	Sewer/Cesspool : _____
Carpet Cleaner: _____	Cleaning Service : _____

- -

Household Safety Information

Location of fire extinguisher(s) : _____

Location of Smoke Detector(s) : _____

Location of Circuit Breaker Panel _____

Location of Water Shut Off Valve _____

Location of Oil Tank _____

Days of Garbage Pick-up _____

Days of Recycle _____

SETTLEMENT CHARGES GUIDE

Below is a list of estimated charges of assorted items or jobs that may sometimes be required after a residence is vacated. All charges are including labor and any parts or materials required. Tenants are not responsible for normal wear and tear, although excessive wear and tear and neglect may incur charges.

CLEANING

Clean refrigerator	50.00
Clean stovetop	30.00
Replace stove drip-bowls	28.00
Clean oven	50.00
Clean stove hood	30.00
Clean kitchen cabinets	45.00
Clean kitchen floor	50.00
Clean tub/shower and surround	30.00 (ea.)
Clean toilet and sink (per bath)	20.00
Clean bathrm.cabinets and floor	25.00
Clean carpets (per room)	75.00
Vacuum throughout dwelling	40.00
Window cleaning(per unit)	11.00
Clean greasy parking spaces	25.00 (ea.)
Clean fireplace	35.00

GENERAL REPAIRS

Replace refrigerator shelf	25.00
Replace stove/oven knob	16.00
Repair ceramic tile	150.00
Replace countertop	275.00
Replace cutting board	40.00
Replace kit/bth cabinet knobs	10.00
Replace mirror	45.00
Replace medicine cabinet	85.00
Replace towel bar	22.00
Replace tub/shower enclosure	195.00
Regrout bath/shower tiles	165.00
Repair porcelain	135.00
Replace thermostat	75.00
Replace fire extinguisher	35.00
Remove junk and debris	250.00
Replace doorbell button	5.00
Replace doorbell unit	50.00
Replace Garage door (each)	525.00

FLOORING

Remove carpet stains	80.00
Deodorize carpet	80.00
Repair carpet	150.00
Repair hardwood floor	95.00
Refinish hardwood floor	380.00
Repair linoleum	85.00
Replace bathroom linoleum	385.00
Replace kitchen linoleum	385.00
Replace floor tile	75.00
Replace ceramic tile	150.00

WALLS

Remove mildew and treat surface	25.00
Cover crayon/marker/pen marks	35.00
Repair hole in wall	55.00
Remove wallpaper	145.00
Repaint (per wall/ceiling)	20.00

DOORS

Repair hole in hollow core door	55.00
Repair forced door damage	75.00
Replace door (inside)	155.00
Replace door (outside)	285.00
Replace sliding glass door	475.00
Replace sliding door screen	55.00

WINDOWS & TREATMENTS

Replace window pane	75.00
Replace Venetian blind	75.00
Replace window shade	15.00
Replace window screen	20.00

LOCKS

Replace key	5.00
Replace door lock	37.00
Replace passage doorlock	18.00
Replace deadbIt lock	18.00

PLUMBING

Replace kitchen faucet	95.00
Replace bathroom faucet	85.00
Replace shower head	24.00
Replace toilet tank lid	25.00
Replace toilet seat	12.00
Replace toilet	165.00
Replace garbage disposer	125.00
Snake Toilet	25.00
Clear sewer/cesspool line	85.00

ELECTRICAL

Replace light bulb	2.50
Replace light fixture globe	12.00
Replace light fixture	55.00
Replace electrical outlet/switch	5.00
Replace electrical cover plate	1.50

GROUNDS / EXTERIOR

Major yard Cleanup	425.00
Minor yard Cleanup	225.00
Mow lawn front and back	50.00
Clean gutters	185.00
Trim bushes	20.00

EXTERMINATING

Exterminate for cockroaches	450.00
Exterminate for fleas	275.00

MAINTENANCE REQUEST & WORK ORDER

UNIT: DATE:

WORK REQUESTED (JOB DESCRIPTION):

_____
_____
_____
_____
_____
_____
_____
_____
_____

CHARGE TO: (CIRCLE ONE)   TENANT   OWNER   MANAGEMENT

ASSIGNED TO:

WORK COMPLETED:

_____
_____
_____
_____
_____
_____
_____

DATE COMPLETED:

APPROVED BY:

IF INCOMPLETE, EXPLAIN:

NOTICE OF PAST DUE RENT

Date: _____

Address: _____

_____

Dear _____,

It's possible you may have overlooked something. Your _____rent payment was

For _____ has not been received. A late charge of $_____ is now due with your payment. According to your rental agreement, an additional daily late charge of $_____ is also due for each day beyond the _____.

Remember, daily late charges can add up. They are an incentive to pay your rent promptly. Please try to avoid them. If you have already sent your rent, but not your late charge, please forward it promptly to avoid additional charges to your account.

Please remit this amount as soon as possible in order to bring your account current and keep your lease in full force. Enclosed is a pre-addressed envelope for your convenience.

Please make all payments payable to: _____

If this matter has been tended to, please disregard this notice and consider it a thank you for your kind
cooperation.

Sincerely,

Manager

NOTICE OF LEASE VIOLATION

TENANT: *Joe Tenant*
ADDRESS: *0000 Bradley Dr. Plainfield, IL. 60544*

DATE: *17 AUG 04*

PLEASE TAKE NOTICE THAT YOU HAVE VIOLATED THE FOLLOWING
COVENANT(S) IN YOUR LEASE RENTAL AGREEMENT:

Section # 41. Vehicles: Vehicles must be both operable and currently registered.

Demand is hereby made that you remedy the noncompliance(s)
within __10__ days of receipt of this notice (by 29 August
2004) or your lease shall be deemed terminated and you shall
vacate the premises upon such termination. If this same
conduct or conduct of a similar nature is repeated within 12
months, your tenancy is subject to termination without your
being given an opportunity to cure the noncompliance.

Please notify Spangler Properties when the violation has been
corrected. An inspector will be sent out to confirm the
violation has been corrected, this will insure your lease is
kept current.

THANK YOU IN ADVANCE FOR YOUR COOPERATION.

SINCERELY,

Spangler Properties, LLC.

Resource List

Web Sites

www.thelpa.com-The Landlord Protection Agency

The LPA is an excellent Web site for beginning real estate investors. I highly recommend becoming a member. The forms and information are well worth the annual membership fee.

www.hud.org-Department of Housing and Urban Development

www.fanniemae.com-Fannie Mae

www.ginniemae.gov-Ginnie Mae

www.freddiemac.com-Freddie Mac

www.va.gov-Veterans Administration

www.vahomes.org-For a listing of homes owned by HUD

www.annualcreditreport.com-For a free copy of your credit report.

Books

Real Estate Riches, by Dolf De Roos (Warner Books)

Flipping Properties, by William Bronchick (Dearborn Trade Publishing)

Landlord's Legal Guide, by Diana Brodman Summers and Mark Warda (Sphinx Publishers)

Financing Secrets of a Millionaire Real Estate Investor, by William Bronchick (Dearborn Trade Publishing)

Real Estate Loopholes, by Diane Kennedy and Garrett Sutton (Warner Books)

Profits, Taxes, & LLCs, by Holmes F. Crouch (Allyear Tax Guides)

How to Profit by Forming Your Own Limited liability Company, by Scott E. Friedman (Upstart Publishing Company)

Cashflow Quadrant, by Robert T. Kiyosaki (Warner Books)

Glossary

Addendum A supplement to a lease that adds or changes the conditions of that lease.

Agreement to Lease A contract stating that a tenant agrees to rent a property from the landlord at some future date.

Amenity An extra item added for convenience such as a refrigerator, stove, garage door opener, etc.

Appraised Value The value of a property based on the value of a similar property in the same surrounding area.

Appreciation The increase in the value of an asset over time.

ARM (Adjustable Rate Mortgage) A loan that has an initial low interest rate which then becomes flexible after a certain period of time has passed.

Arrears An unpaid or overdue debt.

Asset A property with value that is owned or provides cash flow.

Balloon Loan Usually a short term loan where a majority or all of the payment is for interest only causing the payments to be insufficient to pay off the loan in full. The principal amount is due in a lump sum at the end of the loan term.

Capital Gain The profit received from the sale of real estate.

Cash Flow Income from assets.

Closing The transfer of ownership (title) of real estate.

Collateral A property put up to secure a loan.

Common Area An area shared or used by all of the tenants such as a laundry room, stairway, or parking lot.

Condominium (Condo) A multi-unit building in which each unit is owned separately.

Contingency An action that must take place before a contract can be valid or binding.

Conventional Loan Also known as a conforming loan. These loans have specific guidelines to qualify borrowers for loan approvals and can be sold on the secondary market.

Counteroffer A seller rejects an offer made by the buyer and proposes a different offer, which usually benefits the seller.

Depreciation A decrease or loss in value of an asset.

Documentary Tax Stamps (Doc. Stamps) A transfer tax, usually paid by the seller at the closing.

Double Closing The same property is bought and resold in back-to-back closings.

Earnest Money A deposit placed on real estate property as a sign of good faith to purchase.

Encumbrance A lien.

Equity The portion of real estate property that is owned free of debt.

Escrow Extra monies held by the lender to pay property taxes, insurance, and PMI.

Escrow Payment Extra monies taken with the monthly principal and interest payment to hold in a separate account to pay property taxes, insurance, and PMI.

Eviction To have a tenant removed from a rental property by order of the court.

FHA Federal Housing Administration

Flipping Buying and reselling a property in a short period of time.

Foreclosure The legal action of a lender to forcibly acquire property in which a lien was not satisfied.

Freddie Mac (FHLMC) Federal Home Loan Mortgage Corporation.

Ginnie Mae (GNMA) Government National Mortgage Association.

Good Faith Estimate Federal law (RESPA) requires that a statement of the approximate loan and closing costs be provided to the borrower by the lender or broker.

Habitability The rental unit is livable.

Homeowners Association An association that gives homeowners control of the neighborhoods that fall under their association. This helps increase the value of the homes by maintaining the overall appearance of the neighborhood.

HUD Department of Housing and Urban Development.

IOU Written agreement to repay a debt.

Junior Position/Junior Mortgage A lien in the second position on real estate property.

Lease A binding contract between two or more parties permitting the use of property in exchange for rent.

Lease with Option An option can be part of a lease giving the tenant the opportunity to purchase the rental property within a specified period of time. A portion of the monthly rent payment will go towards the down payment for the option. There is also a one-time nonrefundable fee to have the option added.

Lessee Tenant

Lessor Landlord

Liability Debt

LLC Limited Liability Company.

Loan to Value The difference of a property's value and the loan amount.

Mortgage A lien in which the property is placed as collateral.

Mortgage Banker A lender who directly lends its own money.

Mortgage Broker A person who finds a lender for a fee.

Mortgage Insurance (MIP or PMI) Insurance that protects the lender if the borrower defaults. Lenders usually require it if the borrower puts less than 20 percent down of the purchase price.

Mortgagee The lender.

Mortgagor The borrower.

Multiple Listing Service (MLS) A database used by realtors that lists current real estate property that is for sale or has recently been sold.

Net Income/Net Rent Total income after paying operating expenses.

Non-recourse Loan A loan in which the lender can only go after the property or collateral in which they have a lien on to satisfy the loan.

Option to Purchase An option can be part of a lease giving the tenant the opportunity to purchase the rental property within a specified period of time. A portion of the monthly rent payment will go towards the down payment for the option. There is also a one-time nonrefundable fee to have the option added.

PITI Principal, interest, taxes, and insurance.

Plat of Survey A detailed drawing showing a property's boundaries.

Prepayment Penalty A fee in which the lender charges the borrower for paying off a loan early.

Private Mortgage Insurance (PMI or MIP) Insurance that protects the lender if the borrower defaults. Lenders usually require it if the borrower puts less than 20 percent down of the purchase price.

Promissory Note A written agreement to repay a debt.

Quit Claim Deed A deed in which the owner or lien holder legally gives up any rights or ownership in a real estate property.

Recourse Loan The lender can go after the property or collateral and the borrower to satisfy a loan.

Rental Agreement A binding contract between two or more parties permitting the use of property in exchange for rent.

RESPA Real Estate Settlement Procedures Act.

Second Position/Second Mortgage A lien in the second position on real estate property.

Secured Loan A loan backed with collateral.

Service of Process The process of delivering a summons to a defendant of a lawsuit or other legal action.

Settlement Statement A statement listing all closing costs and proceeds to the buyer and the seller. Required by federal law (RESPA).

Sublet To lease real estate property from one party and turn around and rent it to a third party.

Subprime Loan Also known as a nonconforming loan. Lenders who offer this type of loan have their own individual guidelines to approve borrowers.

Summons A notice that legal action has been taken.

Tenancy The period of time in which a property is rented.

Title A document showing proof of ownership.

Title Insurance A policy that protects the lender from discrepancies on the title.

Title Search A search conducted to review the history of ownership on a particular parcel of property.

Truth in Lending A document provided by the lender to the borrower showing loan costs and the interest rate. Required by federal law.

Unsecured Loan A loan that is not backed with collateral.

Warranty Deed A covenant by which the seller guarantees the facts of the title to be correct.

Yield Spread Premium (YSP) The lender pays a commission to the mortgage broker for securing a loan that has an inflated interest rate.